Specter's

What Not to Do

SPAIN

A Unique Travel Guide

Plan your travel with expert advice and Insider Tips: Travel confidently, Avoid Common Mistakes, and indulge in Art, Culture, History, Food, and nature.

Sarah Brekenridge

Table of Contents

Introduction

T he beautiful country of Spain has plenty of things to see and do. It's a country that has captured the imagination of people worldwide, from its vibrant culture to its exciting history, making it a popular destination for travelers seeking adventure, relaxation, or both.

While Spain has a rich history to explore, it also has plenty of things to see and do, especially if you are curious to learn about the stunning medieval, Gothic, and Moorish architecture or want to immerse yourself in one of their many festivals. Spain has hundreds of festivals to enjoy, so there are always various ways to immerse yourself in their culture.

It's an exciting time to plan a trip to a foreign country. However, it can feel equally overwhelming when considering visiting a country with a significant language barrier. In Spain, you can expect that many will speak Spanish. If Spanish is not your first language, it can spark anxiety about going and trying to communicate with others when needed, especially if you're trying to book reservations or get directions. This shouldn't stop you from going! A little preparation can go a long way, even if it means trying to learn basic Spanish phrases (Duolingo is an excellent app for this!).

If you're seasoned in traveling or have never left your home country, you'll know that planning a trip requires plenty of planning and researching. With planning and research come many things you should consider, see, and do. This can understandably feel overwhelming, especially if you plan to be in Spain for no more than 10 days. You can plan your dream trip to Spain, and this book can help you make this trip a reality.

Remember that Spain is a large country with amazing sights and destinations to offer every traveler. Realize now that you likely aren't going to see everything we cover in this book, especially if you intend to find some time to enjoy yourself without cramming your itinerary. There will be plenty of highlights to explore. However, use this book as a helpful source to make the decisions that will fit your trip. The best advice here is to save the things that stand out the most to you so you don't need to juggle all the information.

There is also the concern of when to travel. Spain can get very hot, especially in the summer. So, is there a better time to visit the country? There sure is, and we'll look at those best times so that you can make those decisions as needed.

With Spain being as vibrant of a country as it is, it's understandable that you will want to have as authentic of a trip as possible while avoiding tourist traps or areas that will be overcrowded. In this book, we'll look at the various attractions in many of Spain's cities.

Each chapter has a comprehensive travel guide for Madrid, Barcelona, La Coruna, Salamanca, Cadiz, Grenada, Valencia, and San Sebastian. Each chapter will focus on the highlights and why they are significant to Spain's history and culture so that you can build the trip of a lifetime.

As a traveling enthusiast, I have seen over 200 countries around the globe. I prefer destinations off the beaten path to main tourist attractions to immerse myself in local culture, food, and festivals. Having been to Spain myself, my goal in this book is to help you figure out what your Spain trip will be. Let's get into planning your trip to Spain!

SPAIN

Chapter 1:

Planning   Your   Spanish Adventure

D id you know Spain is the second-largest country in the European Union? If you include their beautiful Canary Islands, Spain is around 195,370 square miles along North Africa's coastline. Thus, it makes sense if you don't know where to start. You may be thinking about cities first, but let's start with the basics before even jumping into the towns and what they offer. It begins with making preliminary plans to get you there.

Uncovering Spain

Much like many of the countries in the European Union, Spain is a different kind of country to visit. With its beautiful castles, monuments, snowcapped mountains, and vibrant cities with its quaint countryside, there is no question why people have loved traveling to this lively and beautiful country.

We could go into an extensive history lesson on Spain, but we'd be here all day if we did because the country's history stems back way before the Romans settled on its land. On that note, Spain is rich in its historical roots, especially with its culture shaped by the Celts and Iberians. However, once the Romans settled in Spain's land, the country was controlled by the Roman Empire.

With Spain's prominent position along the Mediterranean Sea and the Atlantic Ocean, the country was influential in the trading industry. The ability to open up new trading routes on land and sea allowed Spain to become a powerful country by the 16th century, with routes extending to North and South America, Germany, Belgium, France, Italy, the Netherlands, and some areas in North Africa.

Spain has seen plenty of unrest throughout the centuries, including battles with the North African Moors, the Spanish–American War in 1898, and the Spanish Civil War in 1936.

Despite Spain's growth and evolution throughout the centuries, Spain's landscape is diverse. Plenty of mountains in the distance will leave you in awe, with the ranges of Sistema Central and the Montes de Toledo creating a central plateau. However, Spain's natural diversity is significant as the United Nations Educational, Scientific and Cultural Organization (UNESCO) has appointed Spain to have the most biosphere reserves of any country. In Spain, you'll find no shortage of lush green forests to deserts and from sandy beaches to rocky shores with pine trees near the waterline. No matter where you go, you'll be rewarded with picturesque scenery.

While you may expect Spanish to be a prime language in Spain, you will be surprised to learn that it is not the primary spoken tongue. Yes, most of the population will speak Spanish, but it's the second language for most locals— Castilian Spanish is the primary language. Do not fear—if you take the time to learn some basic phrases, you'll find them helpful on your trip.

As for Spain's cultural roots, they're just as diverse thanks to its complex history. Spain's culture is speckled from its blend of earlier influences to give it a vibrant characteristic. Just as Spanish is a widely known language, Spain is also known for its music and dance and how these art forms are a way of expressing emotion. The country's cuisine is fabulous, emphasizing fresh ingredients, bold flavors, and hearty dishes. What you will find on your Spanish adventure is how passionate Spain is about celebrating the spirit, being creative, and living life to the fullest.

Given that Spain has a diverse and rich history, you'll find many landmarks and cities celebrating its rich heritage. You're bound to learn so much about this iconic country and how much it has evolved to where the country is today.

Peak Travel Time to Spain

Spain can be enjoyed year-round. However, in certain seasons, what local events are taking place and whether they will be packed with tourists will decide when the best time for you to go is. Remember, it's your trip! You get to choose when you want to go.

Many may think that Spain is hot all year round, but the climate is relatively mild and dry throughout the year. Winter is cool, but the temperatures rarely dip below 50 °F; however, if you're in Spain during the summer, especially in the southern part of the country, that is where you can expect some scorching days. (But it will make for some good beach days on your vacation!) To better help you plan, here is what to expect temperature-wise and what ideal activities are great for each month:

January: January temperature ranges between 45 and 60 °F. As this is one of the off-season months, this is a great time for sightseeing as it won't be nearly as packed with tourists. Additionally, flights and accommodation tend to be cheaper at this time because not many people are traveling. If you head out to one of Spain's many mountains, you can check out resorts that offer winter sporting activities, such as snowboarding, skiing, or snowshoeing.

February: February temperatures range between 50 to 62 °F. This is still the off-season, so it will make for great sightseeing as it won't be overcrowded with fellow travelers. However, the weather is stormy during February, so pack waterproof clothes and shoes.

March: March temperatures range between 60 and 70 °F. This is only the start of spring, so it won't be overly crowded, making it pleasant to explore the cities and enjoy various outdoor activities, like hiking. You should also expect the weather to be unpredictable.

April: April's temperatures range between 65 and 75 °F. With the warmer air, more restaurants and terraces will open their doors to more patrons, especially in Andalusia. While the weather is starting to warm up, Spain still isn't overly crowded with tourists. It's also a good time for outdoor activities.

May: May starts to heat Spain with temperatures between 70 and 80 °F. This is one of the most beautiful times to go to Spain because of how pleasant the weather is. You can expect plenty of sunny and warm days to explore, with some cooler evenings perfect for fireside tapas.

June: Hello, summer! By June, Spain starts seeing temperatures between 77 and 90 °F. Most days are sunny, so waterproof clothing won't be required. It's still not officially peak season in June, but you can expect more tourists to make their way into the country for their vacations, so museums, beaches, and cathedrals will start to see an uptick in busyness.

July and August: July and August are the height of peak season, with temperatures ranging between 80 to 100 °F—so it is hot! Naturally, the beaches and the patios and terraces will be bustling. Flights and accommodation will also be more expensive if you travel to Spain this month.

September: In September, Spain's peak season winds down, but the temperatures are still relatively warm to hot, reaching between 75 and 90 °F. With the height of tourism starting to wind down, September will allow you to freely explore the country and its landmarks without bumping into people. It will also make hiking and other outdoor excursions more pleasant. September is also a great time to visit Spain if you love wine, as this is when vineyards begin to harvest their grapes, so going on a vineyard tour will be plenty of fun.

October: The temperatures dip between 65 and 75 °F by October. There are fewer tourists in Spain, making visiting landmarks much better. This month is also a great time for surfing in Northern Spain.

November: If you're still looking for other times to visit Spain when it will have less tourism, November is a good time for this. The temperatures range from 55 to 65 °F, so you can expect the air to have a crisp feel.

December: By December, temperatures will range between 45 and 60 °F, and depending on where you are, you may see snow, or it may be warm enough to lounge on the beach. This month is also fun to visit Spain because of the many Christmas festivals.

Flying to Spain Dos and Don'ts

Spain has plenty of major airports that you can fly into:

- A Coruna
- Alicante
- Barcelona
- Bilbao
- Frederico Garcia Lorca
- Girona
- Ibiza
- Lanzarote
- Las Palmas
- Madrid
- Menorca
- Oviedo

- Palma de Mallorca
- Puerto Del Rosario
- Reus
- Santiago
- Sevilla
- Tenerife
- Valencia
- Vigo
- Villanubla
- Zaragoza
- Tenerife—Los Rodeos in the Canary Islands

Most airports are within 12 miles of the city center, easily accessible by taxi, train, or bus.

You can find direct flights there as you research your flights to Spain. These direct flights fly out of

- New York
- Chicago
- Miami
- Los Angeles
- Boston
- Washington, D.C.
- Atlanta
- Dallas

Depending on the time of the year, you may not always find direct flights going into Spain, and you may need to consider a layover. However, direct flights are more regular if you're going to Spain in the summer.

One of the things to keep in mind as you start to look into flights to Spain is if you're willing to be flexible. In other words, is summer the only time you're willing to go, or can you make it work sometime between May and June or September and October? Again, this all comes back to your preferences and whether you're willing to deal with the crowds and hot weather. However, if you're willing to be flexible, this can help with your research. With flexibility in mind, also consider what days you want to fly to Spain. Weekends are understandably more expensive, but you'll likely find something cheaper if you're willing to leave on a Tuesday or Wednesday.

Flight search engines will be your best friend. Google has a great one you can utilize, and it will send you updates on changes and the best deals. If you're not having any luck with Google, Skyscanner and Kayak are other popular options, or you can speak with a travel agent.

As you can see, Spain has a lot of airport options! Of course, the airports in Barcelona and Santiago are likely to be more expensive to fly into because they are major tourist hubs. So, if you're willing to be flexible on where you're flying into, you may want to look at a smaller airport nearby—for example, Reus or Girona, which is close to Barcelona.

When you know your dates, book your flights as early as possible. The earlier you do this, the more cost-efficient it will be. A good rule of thumb for booking is at least six weeks in advance. If you're planning your trip for next year, set an alarm in your phone to start checking or set a Google search alert.

When you have a few options available for flight prices, don't just jump on what looks good—compare prices on multiple websites to ensure you're getting the best deal. However, remember that the cheapest flight may not always be the best option because it may involve lengthy layovers or inconvenient flight times.

Visa and Documentation Requirements

When traveling to Spain for tourism purposes, you can enter the country for up to 90 days within 180 days without a visa. You must ensure your passport is valid beyond three months of your intended stay in the country. If you want to be in Spain longer than three months, you will need the following in addition to a valid passport:

- proof of accommodation
- travel itinerary
- proof of sufficient funds
- medical insurance

It's also important to note that you must complete a health control form before your departure date. It's always best to check with the U.S. Embassy to ensure nothing has changed as you plan for your trip.

Spain Packing Essentials

What to pack for Spain depends on when you're going and what you plan to do. If there is anything I have learned, packing smart means that you pack with comfortable and durable items, opting to wear pieces you can mix and match for your travels. Wearing comfortable shoes is also a must because you'll be doing a lot of it! These items are also must-haves for your traveling needs:

- A rain jacket if you'll be in Spain when the weather is expected to be rainier or unexpected.
- A few comfortable shirts (opt for things you can mix and match).
- A light jacket or sweater for cooler evenings (especially in the spring and autumn).
- A heavier jacket if you'll be in Spain during the cooler months
- If you'll be in Spain during the summer, you'll want to pack some swimwear, shorts, a hat, sunglasses, sandals, and sunscreen.
- Additionally, you will want these items in your luggage:
- an electrical adapter or an electrical converter and adapter combo
- a compact travel umbrella
- a daypack (you can find packable ones on Amazon)
- compressible packing cubes
- a reusable water bottle (Stojo is an excellent brand if you're looking for something that will collapse)
- laundry sheets to do laundry while you travel
- a nice dress
- portable charger
- shawl
- toiletries
- medications (if needed)

It's very easy to overpack! That's why the mix-and-match rule of thumb is essential. Another great rule of thumb is to check the weather a week before your trip. This will give you a better idea of what you need to pack. One of the best ways I figured out how to utilize these is to

- fold your clothes to the size of your packing cube.
- organize and label the days of your outfits. It's a good idea to pack your first three days of outfits in one packing cube and the rest in another. (Remember, if you mix and match, you'll have plenty of options all in one packing cube.)
- use shampoo and conditioner provided in hotel rooms to save space for other toiletries.

Travel Insurance

Many people wonder if travel insurance is worth it, and in all honesty, it is because you never know what could happen that may derail your plans or if something happens to you while you're in Spain. As the saying goes, better safe than sorry!

As you search for travel insurance, you should look for one that will cover everything, not just the basics. You want travel insurance that will cover you if you need to cancel or, if something has interrupted your trip, for any medical expenses, rental car protection, and loss of baggage.

When you buy your travel insurance is also critical. In fact, you should be purchasing it within 15 days of booking your flights or putting a deposit down if you're planning your trip with a tour company. This will ensure you have the early benefits of the travel insurance policy. However, if you want to ensure you get the best deal possible, you can purchase it up to 24 hours before you depart.

If in the event you need to cancel your trip, the cancellation needs to fall under one of these criteria:

- a sudden illness or injury to you, the person you're traveling with, or a family member
- losing your job
- jury duty
- a family emergency
- a transportation strike or other national emergency
- severe inclement weather
- terrorism

When you are ready to purchase your travel insurance, it's vital that you read the fine print. Understand what it is you're buying and what it covers so you don't have any surprises.

Handling All Things Currency

Spain's official currency is the euro (€). When you are traveling abroad, it's always wise to carry a mix of cards and cash for payments. If you plan on bringing cash, you should do it before your departure date. Otherwise, if you decide later you want some cash, there are plenty of ATMs around Spain to do this. However, you might want to double-check with your bank to find out what rates will apply for doing this.

There is also a handy card in Spain called the Wise Euro card. This travel money card will allow you to top up in American dollars, which will be converted to euros to spend. A Wise Euro card guarantees they will give you the best currency rate for euros and is easy to top up.

What Not to Do When Traveling to Spain

Spain is well-loved for its vibrant culture and friendly locals. However, unless you spend a lot of time in one place, you won't necessarily understand the entire culture's etiquette and how people live daily. Check out these pointers that can help you avoid bumps in your trip that can frustrate you.

Don't Try to Shop Between 2 p.m. and 4 p.m.

All throughout Spain, local shops, restaurants, and cafés close their doors for two hours in this block (except major chains and supermarkets). This allows staff at the various establishments to get a mid-day break.

Don't Expect Nights to Be Quiet

With Spain being a highly social country, you can't expect the nights to be quiet—especially if festivals happen. Therefore, it's not uncommon to see people out and about into the wee hours of the morning. You can also expect to hear plenty of traffic throughout, especially if you stay in a city center.

Don't Forget to Check Ahead for Spanish Festivals and Holidays

As mentioned in the previous tip, Spain has a lot of festivals throughout the year. Some of these festivals and holidays are known to inflate prices for tourists looking to travel to Spain. If budget is something you're keeping in mind, check out what festivals and holidays are coming up to ensure you book your trip as far as possible.

Don't Forget to Learn Basic Spanish Phrases

While many people in Spain speak English, especially in tourist areas, it's polite and helpful to learn some basic Spanish phrases. Avoid relying solely on English and make an effort to communicate in Spanish, even if it's just a few words.

Getting Ready for Spain and Beyond

Spain's remarkable history, diverse landscape, and vibrant culture will make for an incredible trip. From its beautiful castles, monuments, snowcapped mountains, and vibrant cities to its quaint countryside, there is no question why people love traveling to this lively and beautiful country.

In this chapter, you've been given all the necessities to start researching your trip to Spain, from considering what season and month you want to go to other vital factors like airports, travel insurance, and money. You've also now got an idea of some pitfalls to avoid when you get to Spain, so you know what to expect. We're just getting started on planning your trip, though!

The next chapter will explore some expert travel tricks and tips for Spain. These hacks help set you up for your trip, no matter where in the country the plane will take you.

Chapter 2:

Tips and Tricks to Explore Spain

Before Spain became the modern-day country we know today, it was once composed of many different kingdoms. By the 15th century, this changed with Isabel of Castile and Fernando of Aragon marrying and bringing their two kingdoms together; thus, Spain began to evolve into the country we are familiar with now.

If that isn't enough of a fun tidbit about Spain, because the country had individual kingdoms throughout, each also spoke its language! Thankfully, with the kingdoms uniting one by one, the language began to evolve—you won't need to worry about communicating in several different ways.

With that said, this chapter will cover many expert tips and tricks for your vacation in Spain, including how to get around and immerse yourself in Spanish culture.

The Ultimate Guide to Spanish Transportation

Spain has plenty of transportation options to suit your needs. However, whatever the mode of transportation you need will depend on your trip requirements and how long you'll be in Spain. Let's explore the various transportation modes that swiftly get you from point A to point B.

By Public Transportation

Spain has made headway in their infrastructure over the past few decades, making it seamless for locals and travelers to move through the cities. If you're not up for renting a car, this might be your best option.

Using the Citymapper app is a great tool to help you navigate Spain's public transportation in the big cities. Alternatively, Google Maps can help you determine which metro options will help you get around the city.

In addition to metro options to get you around, Spain has 12 rapid transit operators in their big cities. They are

- Cercanías Málaga in Málaga
- Rodalies de Catalunya in Catalonia
- Cercanías Bilbao/Bilboko in Aldiriak in Bilbao
- Cercanías Valencia in Valencia
- Cercanías San Sebastián in San Sebastián
- Cercanías Murcia/Alicante in Murcia/Alicante
- Cercanías Cádiz in Cádiz
- Cercanías Zaragoza in Zaragoza
- Cercanías Madrid in Madrid
- Cercanías Asturias in Asturias
- Cercanías Santander in Santander
- Cercanías Sevilla in Sevilla
- Thirteen trams mainly run at street level. They are
- Trambaix, Trambesòs, and Tramvia Blau in Barcelona
- Euskotren Tranbia in Bilbao
- Tranvía de Murcia in Murcia
- Euskotren Tranbia in Vitoria-Gasteiz
- Tranvía Zaragoza in Zaragoza
- Metro Ligero in Madrid
- Tranvía Histórico in A Coruña
- Tranvía de Parla in Parla
- MetroCentro in Sevilla

- Tranvía de Sóller in Sóller
- Alicante TRAM in Alicante
- MetroTenerife in Tenerife
- Metrovalencia in València

Tram, rapid transit, and metro tickets can be purchased at ticket machines at the stops.

By Train

Spain has plenty of railways, including a high-speed train, to get you around the country. Their trains are one of the busiest ways to travel, but they are well-connected to take you to other parts of Spain and Europe. Renfe is the national rail company in Spain. However, they also have regional train companies:

- Euskotren Trena
- Ferrocarril de Sóller
- Ferrocarrils de la Generalitat de Catalunya

Renfe is most likely the option you'll use for train transportation. When booking tickets, you'll need to reserve your ticket time and are sorted by three different fares:

- Basic (básico): This is a standard ticket and does not include cancellations or changes. You can choose your seat for €5.
- Pick and mix (elige): If you miss a train or need to change or cancel, this fare option will give you a discount. Additionally, this ticket includes additional add-ons, including choosing your seat for €5.
- Premium (prémium): This ticket allows you to choose your seat without an additional charge, make changes to who is holding the ticket, and if you need to change when boarding the train or cancel it altogether. You'll also be covered if you miss your train.

If you are looking for train timetables, these are readily available on Catalonia's FGC and Mallorca's FS. Euskotren also has downloadable timetables from their app.

By Bus

There isn't a national bus company in Spain. Instead, each city or urban area runs its own local bus companies with routes in the area. It might feel confusing, so using your phone will be your best friend for navigating the local bus routes. However, the main bus companies in Spain are

- Transports Metropolitans de Barcelona (TMB) in Barcelona
- Guaguas Municipales in Las Palmas de Gran Canaria
- Transportes de Murcia (in Spanish) and TMP Murcia in Murcia
- Consorcio de Transportes del Área de Zaragoza (CTAZ) in Zaragoza
- Bilbobus and BizkaiBus in Bilbao
- Empresa Municipal de Transportes de Madrid (EMT Madrid) in Madrid
- Consorcio de Transporte Metropolitano del Área de Málaga (CTMAM) in Málaga
- Empresa Municipal de Transportes de Palma de Mallorca (EMT Palma) in Palma
- Transportes Urbanos de Sevilla (TUSSAM) in Sevilla
- Empresa Municipal de Transportes de València (EMT València) in València

Bus prices will vary based on the operating company. However, some may offer a 10-trip ticket or a 24-hour ticket as well. You can also expect many of the transport companies to provide contactless payments instead of having to manage paper tickets.

Long-distance coach buses are also an option, but there are not as many available as you might find by taking trains. Alsa and Avanza are the two companies covering Spain's peninsula coast. However, you can also look into Coms, Hife, Daibus, Damas, and Interbus if you need a bus to take you further. Tickets for these buses can be bought at the station, on the bus, or through their website.

By Taxis or Uber

Taxis are available in any part of Spain and can quickly be hired if you're at a central transportation hub. However, you can also flag one down if needed. Paying by cash is easier if you're taking a cab. But if you don't have cash, verify they can take a credit card. Most base fares are charged by the kilometer between €1 and €2, with a base fare between €2 and €3.

You can also use a taxi app to call a cab. The leading apps for this in Spain are

- Cabify
- FREE NOW
- TaxiClick

Uber is also an option in Spain if that is a preference.

By Plane

Since Spain isn't a tiny country, you may want to consider traveling by plane. Iberia, Air Europa, Volotea, and Vueling are the leading airlines that offer plenty of domestic routes and will fly into

- Adolfo Suárez Madrid-Barajas Airport
- Barcelona-El Prat Airport
- Palma de Mallorca Airport
- Málaga-Costa del Sol Airport

By Ferry

If you want to go and explore one of Spain's islands, the best way to get there is by taking a ferry. Spain has many ferry options from the mainland to take you to the Balearic Islands, the Canary Islands, Melilla, and Ceuta.

Spain Travel Safety Tips

Traveling to a different country is always exciting. But when it's out of your normal routine, you may try to think of ways to keep yourself safe. Spain is safe, but it's also good to be mindful of a few things to ensure your trip is enjoyable.

Crime Rates

Compared to other European countries, Spain's crime rate is relatively low. If anything, petty theft and pickpocketing are two things you should look out for (as you would in your home city). While on public transportation, remember to keep your items close to you so a thief won't grab them and run off. If you rent a car, keep the doors locked when you park and take anything valuable with you. Remember to lock up your passports and other valuable items in the safe if you stay in a hotel.

Be on the Lookout for Scams

There are a couple of scams to be on the lookout for while traveling around Spain. They are the Trileros scam and the Rosary gift scam.

The trailer scam, or the shell scam, involves a street performer placing small objects under a shell or a cup. They will then mix the shells or cups up and ask the spectators to guess which has a specific item. The chances of you guessing correctly aren't the point. You and other spectators are focused on what the street performer is doing, leaving you vulnerable to petty left.

In the rosemary gift scam, you may get approached by a gypsy to offer you a rosemary as a gift. She may even grab your palm to read it. This is a ploy to distract you while someone else she knows pickpockets from you. She may demand money from you if she doesn't have an accomplice. The best thing you can do is say, "No gracias," and walk away.

Emergency and Embassy Services Numbers

If you ever require emergency services, the emergency number to dial is 112. This number will cover all emergencies, including accidents, risk situations, and medical issues.

Spain has three U.S. Embassies to serve you in the event you need assistance such as a lost or stolen passport:

- U.S. Embassy in Madrid: Calle de Serrano, 75, 28006 Madrid, Spain
- U.S. Embassy in Barcelona: Paseo Reina Elisenda de Montcada, 23, 08034 Barcelona, España
- U.S. Embassy in Palma de Mallorca: Carrer de Porto Pi, 8, Ponent, 07015 Palma, Illes Balears

Traveling Solo

So many people, myself included, love to travel solo. It's a thrilling experience as you immerse yourself in places beyond your comfort zone. But it also means you should be more aware of your surroundings to ensure your solo travels stay stress-free.

One of the first things you should do is to research and plan for where you will be. This will give you the time to get an idea of the surroundings in the areas you plan to visit and stay. As you research, you should be looking for hotels or hostels in safe neighborhoods.

When you arrive in Spain and are traveling, always be aware of your surroundings and keep an eye on your belongings, especially if you're traveling through busier parts of the city or when areas are crowded; this also applies to traveling on public transportation or trains. If you're out at night, avoid walking in poorly lit areas.

Lastly, share your itinerary with your family and provide important documents so they know where you will be.

Natural Disasters

Since Spain has a diverse landscape, natural disasters can occur while traveling. It's always best to watch for any significant weather reports, especially if it involves potential flooding or severe thunderstorms.

If you're traveling to Spain during the summer months, expect heat waves to happen. Be sure to find plenty of shaded spots, and carry a water bottle to keep yourself hydrated.

What Not to Do When Traveling Around Spain

Don't Forget to Look in to Small Rental Cars

While you have transportation options around Spain, it doesn't hurt to consider renting a car, even a small one! If you pack light, a small car shouldn't be an issue to get you around the various destinations in Spain (plus it's another excellent way to explore the country).

Don't Forget About Toll Roads

Spain has plenty of toll roads connecting you to different cities, so don't be surprised if you must pay as you drive from one place to the next. As such, you'll want to ensure you have some change handy, as most don't take cards.

The prices at each toll will vary depending on how long you're driving on the road. However, most tolls are no more than €15.

Don't Ignore Pickpocketing Risks

Tourist areas in Spain, especially in large cities like Barcelona and Madrid, are known for pickpocketing. Avoid carrying large amounts of cash or valuables in crowded places, and keep your belongings secure at all times, especially in tourist hotspots and on public transportation.

Respecting Spanish Culture

As Spain is a popular tourist destination with various regions, you'll notice that each area has its unique culture and traditions. Utilize these tips to help you immerse yourself deeper into their culture.

Do Try to Learn Some Spanish

You don't need to be fluent in Spanish, but the locals will appreciate your attempts to communicate with them in Spanish. These key phrases are a great starting point:

- Buenos días: Good morning
- Buenas tardes: Good afternoon
- Buenas noches: Good evening
- Hola: Hello
- ¿Cómo estás? How are you?

Do Try Tapas

Tapas in Spain is a must-try. These small portions are a great way to try some of Spain's traditional foods.

Do Expect Siesta Hours to Be Quiet

Spain's mid-day break allows the locals to unwind and recharge for the rest of the day. It is a strange concept to foreigners but sacred to the Spaniards. During the siesta, this is the time when Spaniards will take their lunch or do whatever else they need to find that work-life balance.

Do Expect to Eat Late

Since the Siesta has businesses and restaurants close for two hours in the middle of the day for lunch, many restaurants will re-open around 8 p.m. So, if you are looking to eat out, you should expect to eat later than expected.

Do Mind Your Volume

Do mind your volume while out in and about or dining in a restaurant or café. Spaniards prefer a quieter environment, especially during siesta.

Don't Ignore Regional Differences

As every region of Spain differs, expect some areas to follow different cultural etiquette. It is good to do more profound research into cultural aspects that make the region or regions you visit unique.

Don't Feel Pressured to Tip at Restaurants

When dining at a restaurant, don't feel the need to tip. Servers are paid living wages, so you're only expected to tip if you eat with a large group or in a higher-scale restaurant with excellent service. If you tip in that scenario, don't leave more than 10%.

Don't Wear Beachwear if You're Not at the Beach

Spanish culture and customs expect people to be modestly dressed unless they're headed to the beach. Wear a dress, pants, or shorts over your swimwear when leaving the beach.

Don't Be Easily Offended

You may come across a blunt Spaniard from time to time. Don't get offended, as it's a part of their culture. It's not their intention to step on your toes.

Don't Bring Up Bullfighting

Bullfighting is a controversial topic in Spain that can ignite strong emotions from people. If the conversation arises, be open-minded and seek to understand.

Let's Start Exploring

Getting around Spain is easy with its well-connected transportation system, which has many options to cater to your traveling needs within a city and from one to another. These tips should help you plan so you can build your dream vacation itinerary without any worry.

You've also learned about the customs that make Spain unique. Keep these tips in mind as you interact with the locals to ensure you can immerse yourself within the locals rather than standing out like a tourist.

Now that we have covered the different transport methods, how to keep yourself safe, and the ins and outs of Spanish etiquette, let's turn our attention to exploring Madrid. Madrid is Spain's capital city and one of the country's most vibrant and diverse cities. In the next chapter, we will explore the best things to do in Madrid, including some great attractions, eateries, festivals, where to stay, and what not to do.

Chapter 3:

Madrid—Dos and Don'ts

Do you know the origins of Madrid's history? Madrid's vibrant city and surrounding land have been home to inhabitants since the Stone Age. However, the town was established in the ninth century when Muhammad I of Cordoba decided to build the Royal Palace of Madrid overlooking the Manzanares River. The castle still stands here today and is one of the places we will look at for your adventures around this beautiful city.

Discovering Madrid

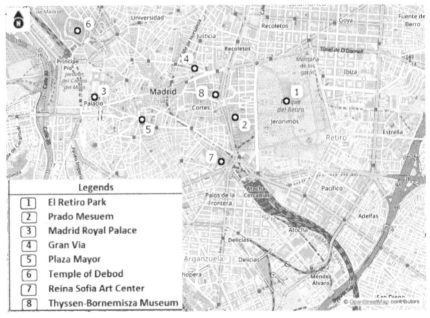

Legends	
1	El Retiro Park
2	Prado Mesuem
3	Madrid Royal Palace
4	Gran Via
5	Plaza Mayor
6	Temple of Debod
7	Reina Sofia Art Center
8	Thyssen-Bornemisza Museum

Madrid is Spain's capital with plenty of rich history to discover. However, although its rich history dates back to the Stone Age and the Royal Palace was built in the ninth century, it didn't become Spain's capital until the 16th century when King Phillip II moved his wife and their court from Toledo to the new capital city. Some believe King Phillip II's wife hated Toledo's climate, though it has never been confirmed if this was the reason for the move.

Nonetheless, Madrid is in the heart of Spain and the center of the Iberian Peninsula. Because the city has a high altitude, Madrid has a unique climate and landscape. Madrid is renowned for its celebrated cuisine, boasting regional and international dishes and many landmarks that attract thousands of visitors yearly. Let's explore the things to do while in Madrid.

What to Do in Madrid

El Retiro Park

Address: Plaza de la Independencia 7

Hours of operation

* Spring to fall: 6 a.m. to 12 a.m.
* Winter: 6 a.m. to 10 p.m.

El Retiro Park is a stunning park covering over 350 acres of land in the center of Madrid. Originally a royal garden to the former Old Buen Retiro Palace, this beautiful park opened in 1868 and has since become one of Madrid's most popular destinations for locals and tourists alike to spend a few hours in. Along with its expansive green space and beautiful winding pathways to wander, El Retiro Park is home to various attractions, including the stunning Crystal Palace, made entirely of glass, and the beautiful Rosaleda rose garden, which features over 4,000 rose bushes.

While you explore El Retiro, it is worth paying a visit to the Great Pond, one of the oldest monuments in the park, dating back to the 17th century. Though it once was the place for naval battle shows and a way for the former Kings of Spain to enjoy their time, today, visitors can enjoy a relaxing boat ride or stroll around the stalls that pop up here on the weekends.

As this is a public park, there is no admission fee to the park or the Crystal Palace. However, if you want to rent a boat, it is €6 from Monday to Friday and €8 on Saturdays and Sundays. You can easily reserve your boat using the Madrid Movil app.

Prado Museum

Address: Paseo del Prado s/n 28014 Madrid

Hours of operation

- Monday to Saturday: 10 a.m. to 8 p.m.
- Sundays and holidays: 10 a.m. to 7 p.m.
- Closed on January 1, May 1, and December 25
- Limited opening hours on January 6 and December 24 and 31

The Prado Museum is one of Madrid's most important museums anyone should visit, whether you're an enormous art enthusiast or not. The Prado Museum contains an impressive number of masterpieces from various artists, including the works of Pedro Berruguete, Fray Juan Bautista Maíno, Raphael, Georges De La Tour, El Greco, and Vincente López Portaña.

Ticket type	Price
General Admission	€ 15
Seniors (65 years old and up)	€ 7.50
Children under 18 or students up to 25 years old	Free
Add an audio guide	€ 5
Guided tour ticket	€ 10
General admission and a copy of the "Prado guide."	€ 24
Art walk pass	€ 32
Private visits (from 9 a.m. to 10 a.m.)	€ 50

For a money-saving trick, visit Prado Museum during their free hours from 6 p.m. to 8 p.m. Monday to Saturday and 5 p.m. to 7 p.m. on Sundays and holidays.

Royal Palace of Madrid

Address: C. de Bailén, s/n, Centro, 28071 Madrid

Hours of operation

- October to March:
  - Monday to Friday: 10 a.m. to 6 p.m.
  - Sunday: 10 a.m. to 4 p.m.
- April to September:
  - Monday to Friday: 10 a.m. to 7 p.m.
  - Sunday: 10 a.m. to 4 p.m.
- The last admission is one hour before closing. Hours are subject to change based on holidays.

As you recall, the Royal Palace of Madrid is Europe's largest and oldest palace, dating back to the ninth century. However, the original palace sadly burned down. You will visit the reconstructed castle in Madrid, commissioned by King Phillip V in 1734. On the outside, this stunning castle boasts a grand entrance with limestone statues of more than 44 Spanish royals, but the inside will leave you in awe. There are more than 3,000 rooms throughout the six-floor castle. Even though you will only get to explore around a dozen of the rooms, standing inside alone will give you an idea of how magnificent the Royal Palace is. This is a great way to steep yourself into some of the oldest history of Madrid.

The tour of the Royal Palace is self-guided, and you can rent an audio guide for an additional fee. This must be arranged at their box office if you want to take a guided tour. Otherwise, it's best to pre-book your tickets online.

Ticket type	Price
General Admission	€ 20
Reduced admission (5 to 16 years old, seniors 65 and up, and students up to 25 years old)	€ 13
Visitors with disabilities	Free
Add an audio guide	€ 3

All tickets come with management fees of €0.77 on top of the price.

Gran Vía

Strolling along Madrid's well-known street, Gran Vía, is a must. This street dates back to 1862 when Madrid's city center was being renovated, though construction of the street did not begin until 1910 and was completed by 1929.

Along the Gran Vía, there are several bars, restaurants, and shops to stop into. This is the place to be if you want to enjoy some nightlife action.

Plaza Mayor

Address: Plaza Mayor 28012

The Plaza Mayor is Madrid's famous public square in the heart of the city, known for its distinctive architecture, with several buildings featuring beautiful balconies and ornate facades.

The history of the Plaza Mayor dates back to the 17th century when it opened in 1620. This square has hosted many events, including bullfights, fiestas, and processions. This is a great place to soak up the sun, grab a bite to eat, or enjoy a coffee while watching the hustle and bustle. If you're in Madrid before Christmas, a Christmas market is also here, perfect for picking up a unique gift.

Temple of Debod

Address: C. de Ferraz, 1, Moncloa-Aravaca, 28008 Madrid

Hours of operation: 10 a.m. to 8 p.m. from Tuesday to Sunday. Closed every Monday and on January 1 and 6, May 1, and December 24, 25, and 31. The last admission time is at 7:30 p.m.

It's interesting to see an Egyptian temple in Madrid, but the Temple of Debod is worth visiting, especially since it's a free attraction. This temple dates back to the second century and was built near Aswan by the Nile River. It was created to honor the god Amun and the goddess Isis.

The temple was moved to Madrid sometime in the 1960s when higher water levels threatened to cause irreparable damage. Instead of allowing it to be destroyed, the Egyptian government gifted the temple to Spain as a "thank you" for their help in restoring other ancient temples in the country. As such, the Temple of Debod was deconstructed and moved to the Parque del Oeste.

The Golden Triangle

The Golden Triangle in Madrid contains three fantastic art museums. They are the Museo Del Prado (Prado Museum, which we covered earlier), Museo Nacional Arte Reina Sofia (Reina Sofia Art Center), and the Museo Nacional Thyssen-Bornemisza (Thyssen-Bornemisza National Museum).

These museums contain some of the best art collections in Spain, some going as far back as 500 years ago to more recent artists from the 20th century. Visiting one or all of these museums is perfect for any art enthusiast or immersing yourself in some of Spain's art history.

Reina Sofia Art Centre

Address: C. de Sta. Isabel, 52, Centro, 28012 Madrid

Hours of operation: Open Monday and Wednesday to Saturday from 10 a.m. to 9 p.m. and Sunday from 10 a.m. to 2:30 p.m.

Museum access is free from 7 p.m. to 9 p.m. on Monday and Wednesday to Saturday and from 12:30 p.m. to 2:30 p.m. on Sundays.

The Reina Sofia Art Center is the art gallery to visit if you want to view contemporary art from the 20th century. Here, you'll see the works of Pablo Picasso, Salvador Dalì, and Joan Mirò.

Ticket type	Price
General Admission	€12
Combined ticket	€16.50

Combined tickets include a joint visit to the Collection and the temporary exhibits.

Thyssen-Bornemisza National Museum

Address: Paseo del Prado, 8, 28014 Madrid
Hours of operation
- Monday: 12 p.m. to 4 p.m.
- Tuesday to Sunday: 10 a.m. to 7 p.m.

The Thyssen-Bornemisza Museum is home to one of the largest private art collections in the world, with over 1,000 works of art in their permanent collection. You will see many of Europe's renowned artists at this museum, including Duccio, Rembrandt, and Paolo Uccello. The Thyssen-Bornemisza Museum also hosts temporary exhibits throughout the year to showcase the works of emerging and established artists.

Ticket type	Price
General Admission	€ 13
Seniors (65 years old and up) and students	€ 9
Children under 18	Free
Add on an audio guide	€ 5
Group tickets (for up to six people)	€ 11

If you visit this museum on a Monday, the admission is free.

What Festivals to Enjoy in Madrid

The Virgin of La Almudena Festival

The Virgin of La Almudena is Madrid's patron saint, honored every year on November 9. This religious festival includes musical performances and traditional dances. The festival's highlight is the procession, which involves carrying the Virgin of La Almudena statue along the Plaza Mayor and Plaza de la Almudena after a mass and an offering of flowers in the morning. This festival is a great way to immerse yourself in Madrid's culture and traditions.

Semana Santa

Easter on our side of the country is often celebrated with chocolate and the Easter Bunny. However, in Spain, Semana Santa is a holy week that precedes Easter Sunday. While there won't be any chocolate eggs, this festival offers a fantastic opportunity for travelers to explore and witness many of Madrid's iconic attractions, providing insight into the sacredness of Easter in Spain.

Semana Santa commences on Palm Sunday, and throughout the week, captivating daily parades take place. One of these parades, the procession of silence, is particularly noteworthy as worshippers walk in complete silence, creating an eerie yet beautiful atmosphere.

If you're seeking delicious traditional cuisine, some Semana Santa sweets are worth trying (even if they aren't chocolate). Don't miss out on the torrija, a sweet treat similar to French toast. And if you prefer savory dishes, try soldaditos de pavía (crispy cod).

Regardless of how you spend Semana Santa, there are numerous ways to fully immerse yourself in this religious week and understand why this holiday holds such sacred significance in Spain.

Dos de Mayo

Dos de Mayo (The Day of Madrid) happens each year on the second of May. During this yearly celebration, Madrid celebrates the uprising against Napoleon's troops in 1808. The rebellion was sparked by the news that the French intended to imprison the Spanish royal children and take them to France and was met with fierce resistance from the locals. Despite being outnumbered, the people of Madrid fought against the French troops, determined to defend their country.

While not much was achieved from the initial rebellion, this became a symbol of Spanish resistance to fight foreign domination and ultimately led to the Spanish War of Independence when the rebellion inspired other acts of uprising around the country. The war lasted six years and ended with Spain gaining independence on April 17, 1814.

Today, the Dos de Mayo holiday is a day of celebration with many parades, concerts, and other cultural events to immerse yourself in. This is a great day to learn more about Spain's rich history and a day to remember the bravery and sacrifice of the Spanish people who fought back. You'll get a feel for how proud the people of Madrid are everywhere that day!

La Paloma

If you are in Madrid in the middle of August, the La Paloma festival is worth experiencing. This festival honors the Virgin of La Paloma, a painting in the Church of San Pedro el Real. This festival is known for its colorful and lively atmosphere, with people dressed in traditional costumes dancing in the streets and enjoying live music and performances. In addition, the Virgin of La Paloma painting is taken into procession through Madrid's streets after flowers and mass are offered in the morning. This festival is a ton of fun and worth experiencing if you're in Madrid when the festival is happening.

Where to Eat in Madrid

Madrid has many great options for eating out, but many might be at a higher price point. However, as the saying goes, you only live once, so why not give one of these restaurants a go?

Tripea

Address: Calle Vallehermoso, 36 (Puesto 44 del Mercado), 28015 Madrid, Comunidad de Madrid

The markets throughout Madrid are constantly changing to attract the next generation of people. Tripea is a stall in Mercado de Vallehermoso and is an inviting experience. Chef Roberto Martínez Foronda invites his guests to sit at a communal table overlooking his tiny open kitchen, where you can enjoy a fusion of food, from traditional Spanish to Asian and Latin flavors.

To enjoy this experience, you must make a reservation for 2:30 p.m. or 9:30 p.m.

DiverXO

Address: Calle Padre Damián, 23, 28036, Madrid, Comunidad de Madrid

DiverXO is not just a place to eat—it's a wild experience with the kitchen headed by the brilliant chef David Muñoz. DiverXO is Madrid's only three Michelin-star restaurant, and your dining experience here will be full of surprise and amazement with his creative cooking skills. This restaurant only offers a tasting menu and will be the most expensive option. But, if you have the wiggle room in the budget for something to wow you, this is the place. Reservations must be made in advance, starting at €395 per person (including drinks).

Casa Dani

Address: Calle Ayala, 28, 28001 Madrid, Comunidad de Madrid

Casa Dani is the place to go if you want to try the tortilla española. This delicious potato and egg dish is hearty, comforting, and a popular option among the patrons. If you plan to eat here at lunch, expect it to fill up, so try to get a spot by 11 a.m.!

Los Montes de Galicia

Address: Calle Azcona 46, 28028 Madrid

Los Montes de Galicia is a popular dining option in Madrid if you're looking to enjoy some classic Galician dishes and modern Spanish cuisine. Patrons of this restaurant rave about its fantastic service and the eclectic range of desserts. This is a mid-to-higher-range restaurant, but you'll leave with a satisfied belly.

Lakasa

Address: Plaza del Descubridor Diego de Ordás, 1, Madrid 28003

At Lakasa, allow chef César Martín to delight your taste buds with his delicious Spanish delicacies infused with a twist using French and Mediterranean flavors. For the low-to-mid range price point, you'll be equally surprised at how excellent the service is in this restaurant. Servers will pour you generous glasses of wine as you peruse the menu with at least 20 regular dishes and seasonal ones. You can do full or half-size, which is perfect if you want to try a few things.

What to Eat in Madrid

Bocadillo de Calamares:

A quintessential Madrid street food, the bocadillo de calamares is a sandwich filled with crispy calamari rings. Often enjoyed with a squeeze of lemon, this simple yet tasty snack is a local favorite.

Cocido Madrileño:

Cocido Madrileño is a hearty stew that reflects the comfort food of Madrid. It typically consists of chickpeas, vegetables, chorizo, morcilla (blood sausage), and various cuts of pork. It is served in multiple courses, starting with the broth and chickpeas, followed by the meats and vegetables.

Patatas Bravas:

Patatas Bravas is a classic Spanish tapa, and in Madrid, you'll find some of the best. These crispy, fried potato cubes are served with a spicy tomato sauce (brava sauce) and often accompanied by aioli or other flavorful sauces.

Jamón Ibérico:

Spain is famous for its cured ham, and Jamón Ibérico is a prized delicacy. Savor thin slices of this high-quality, acorn-fed Iberian ham, which boasts a unique flavor and texture. Many tapas bars in Madrid offer Jamón Ibérico as part of their menu.

Churros con Chocolate:

Indulge in a sweet treat by trying churros con chocolate. These deep-fried dough pastries are often enjoyed for breakfast or as a snack. Dip the churros in thick, rich hot chocolate for a delicious and comforting experience.

Where to Stay in Madrid

As Madrid has plenty of cultural landmarks to explore, it's easy to see why this vibrant city is famous for travelers. Of course, with so many things to experience, Madrid has excellent accommodations for your traveling needs, from palaces to hybrid hotels with art galleries and everything in between.

Most hotels and other accommodation options are scattered around the middle of the city. But if you don't want to stay right in the center of the action, there are plenty of places just outside the busy city center.

Mercure Madrid Centro

Address: Lope de Vega, 49, Madrid City Center, 28014 Madrid

Mercure Madrid Centro is a great accommodation option if you're looking for places to explore the city. This mid-range hotel is conveniently near a metro station that can take you anywhere in the town near museums and galleries.

Hotel Mexico

Address: Gobernador, 24, Madrid City Center, 28014 Madrid

For budget-friendly accommodation options, check out Hotel Mexico. This hotel is near El Retiro Park and Madrid's Botanic Gardens, among other nearby attractions.

Hostal Retiro

Address: O'Donnell, 27, Salamanca, 28009 Madrid

If traveling to Spain solo, you should consider staying at the Hostal Retiro. This hostel is near El Retiro Park, several museums, and a bus stop to efficiently get you around the city for your exploring needs.

Vincci the Mint

Address: Gran Vía 10, Madrid City Center, 28013 Madrid

Vincci the Mint is a great mid-range hotel if you want to be in Madrid's heart. This stylish hotel has a unique and modern design, incorporating the color of mint throughout the property. Inside the rooms, you'll find them spacious and comfortable to relax after a day of exploring the city. Additionally, Vincci the Mint has a rooftop terrace offering a stunning panoramic view of the city, perfect for those summer evenings!

Holiday Inn Express Madrid Airport

Address: Avenida de Aragón, 402, Ciudad Pegaso, Madrid 28022

The Holiday Inn Express is always a great option, especially if you're looking for something budget-friendly, want to stay out of the hustle and bustle of the city, or if Madrid is last on your list of cities to visit in Spain and want to be near the airport. This accommodation has all the basics, including a gym, a pool, and a restaurant. Breakfast is included in your hotel fee as well.

H10 Puerta de Alcalá

Address: Alcala, 66, Madrid 28009

You'll find great comfort in the rooms at the H10 Puerta de Alcalá, which have fantastic city views. This hotel offers plenty of room options to suit your needs, including small family rooms. H10 Puerta de Alcalá also has a pool onsite and includes breakfast with your room fee, which is about mid-range.

Hotel Nuevo Boston

Address: Avenida de Aragon 332, Madrid, 28022

At the upscale Hotel Nuevo Boston, you'll find yourself central to several attractions in Madrid, many of which are within walking distance or a short drive from the hotel. This hotel has many room options, including family rooms, standard double, and triple twin rooms. They also have a pool and free airport shuttles.

Melia Madrid Princesa

Address: Princesa 27, Madrid, Madrid, 28008

Melia Madrid Princesa puts you in Madrid's heart, offering a five-star service at a mid-range price. This hotel has plenty of amenities to serve your needs, including a spa, gym, and an indoor pool. The Melia Madrid Princesa is a 14-minute walk from the Royal Palace of Madrid and a short drive to the Plaza Mayor.

The Madrid EDITION

Address: Plaza de Celenque 2, Madrid 28013

The Madrid EDITIoN is a luxury option in the heart of Madrid, putting you within walking distance of several attractions, including the El Retiro Park. This hotel boasts a sophisticated and stylish interior, with stunning furnishings in each room and the lobby. Their restaurant is also stunning inside, making you feel like you've entered a secret Spanish garden. As you can expect, this hotel is higher-end, but the staff will ensure your stay with them is memorable and comfortable!

Mandarin Oriental Ritz

Address: Plaza de la Lealtad 5, 28014 Madrid

Luxury meets exceptional service at the Mandarin Oriental Ritz. In this hotel, you will feel like you've stepped back into the Roaring Twenties with the stunning interior of the lobby and main floor. This hotel has 100 rooms and 53 suites, boasting natural light and space, making it feel like home. You can also have butler service if you want to go a little extra. Of course, with this being a Ritz hotel, it is genuinely the highest-end experience, but worth it if you want to splurge.

What Not to Do in Madrid

While visiting Madrid, utilize these tips to ensure you stay safe.

Don't Become Too Distracted

Although Madrid's crime rate is relatively low, it's easy to become distracted by your surroundings. Be mindful of what is going on and ensure you keep your belongings close to you, especially if you are exploring these areas: The Gran Vía, Puerta del Sol, and El Rastro Market

Don't Go to These Neighborhoods

Every city has its rough areas, and while Madrid is a safe city, you're best to stick to the central area and avoid these neighborhoods that have higher gang and violent rates:

- Villaverde
- Usera
- Orcasur
- Pan Bendito
- Puente de Vallecas
- San Blas

Don't Underestimate the Heat

Madrid can get very hot, especially in the summer months. Avoid underestimating the heat, and ensure you stay hydrated by carrying a water bottle and wearing appropriate clothing and sunscreen.

Don't Miss out on the Tapas Culture

Madrid is known for its lively tapas scene, with numerous bars and taverns offering a wide variety of small plates. Avoid missing out on this quintessential Madrid experience by not indulging in tapas hopping. Embrace the tradition of enjoying small bites with friends and locals.

Don't Miss out on Purchasing Tickets in Advance

Many popular tourist attractions in Madrid, such as the Prado Museum and Royal Palace, can have long queues, especially during peak tourist seasons. Avoid waiting in line by purchasing tickets in advance online or through authorized ticket vendors.

Don't Ignore Opening and closing hours

Check the opening hours of the attractions you plan to visit and avoid arriving outside of these times. Some attractions may have limited hours on certain days or be closed for holidays or maintenance.

Don't Skip Guided Tours

Consider taking guided tours of major tourist attractions, especially if you're interested in learning more about the history, architecture, or cultural significance of the site. Avoid missing out on valuable insights by exploring attractions on your own.

Don't Forget to Carry Necessary Supplies

Depending on the attraction and the time of year, it's essential to bring necessary supplies such as water, sunscreen, and comfortable walking shoes. Avoid discomfort or dehydration by being prepared for your visit.

Don't Forget to Check on Special Events or festivals

Some tourist attractions in Madrid host special events, exhibitions, or temporary installations that may enhance your visit. Avoid missing out on these unique experiences by checking for upcoming events or exhibitions before your visit.

Next Stop: Barcelona

Madrid is undoubtedly a city of rich history, culture, and beauty, with many things to explore and discover. This is just the start of your planning, and while Madrid is relatively central in the country, going to Barcelona is also worth exploring and is just a short train ride away. Barcelona is known for many things, from its stunning architecture to beautiful beaches and much more! Let's explore some things you should do in this iconic city.

Chapter 4:

Barcelona—Dos and Don'ts

SPAIN

Barcelona's origins are mysterious. Some romantics believe this historic city was founded by Hercules centuries before the Romans inhabited this part of Spain. Others believe it was built by the Carthaginian general Hamilcar Barca, who was Hannibal's father. While it's unclear how Barcelona came to be, there is much to see!

Legends

1	Basilica de la Sagrada Familia
2	Barri Gothic
3	Palau de la Musica Catalana
4	Museu Picasso de Barcelona
5	Catedra de la Sana Cruz
6	Bogatell Beach
7	Casa Mila

Discovering Barcelona

Barcelona is everything you expect it to be and more. This city, which dates back to Roman times, is rich in history and well-loved for its beautiful beaches and quaint streets. Most people in Barcelona speak Catalan, which you'll hear plenty of if you attend their cultural festivals. Exploring Barcelona will allow you to discover celebrated landmarks such as the Sagrada Família, the Palau, and Casa Mila.

What to Do in Barcelona

Barcelona has plenty of noteworthy landmarks to explore. Consider exploring some of these monuments while in Barcelona!

Basílica de la Sagrada Família

Address: C/ de Mallorca, 401, L'Eixample, 08013 Barcelona

Hours of operation

- November to February
  - Monday to Saturday: 9 a.m. to 6 p.m.
  - Sunday: 10:30 a.m. to 6 p.m.
- March and October
  - Monday to Saturday: 9 a.m. to 7 p.m.
  - Sunday: 10:30 a.m. to 7 p.m.
- April to September
  - Monday to Saturday: 9 a.m. to 7 p.m.
  - Sunday: 10:30 a.m. to 7 p.m.
- Special hours of operation
  - December 25 and 26 and January 1 and 6: 9 a.m. to 2 p.m.

The Basílica de la Sagrada Família (primarily called Sagrada Família) is Barcelona's Roman Catholic church. Construction began in 1874 after a group campaigned for a new church to honor the Holy Family. Many years went into planning this magnificent church, and the first cornerstone was laid on March 19, 1882.

As you will see if you visit, this cathedral is incomplete. However, it is a stunning piece of architecture on the outside and inside, with tall columns and large stained-glass windows allowing sunlight in. You can also climb the towers, seeing panoramic views of Barcelona from 65 meters up.

When visiting Sagrada Familía, please keep in mind their dress code:

- Visitors cannot wear see-through clothing or swimwear or have their shoulders showing.
- Pants, shorts, and skirts must come at least mid-thigh.
- Visitors cannot wear clothing that celebrates festivities or draws attention.

All tickets can be bought at Sagrada Familía, but based on what is available, it's better to prebook online to avoid disappointment. You can purchase tickets up to two months before visiting. Also, your ticket time is firm. If you show up late, you won't be able to enter the basilica.

Individual Self-Guided Tour

Ticket type	Price
General admission	€ 26
Students or visitors under 30 years old	€ 24
Seniors	€ 21
Children under 11 years old	Free
Mass	Free

Sagrada Família With Guided Tour

Ticket type	Price
General admission	€ 30
Students or visitors under 30 years old	€ 28
Seniors	€ 23
Children under 11 years old	Free

Sagrada Familia With a Guide and Visit to the Towers

During this tour, you'll join one of Sagrada Família's experts, who will give you a more in-depth history of this cathedral and some of its best-kept secrets. You'll also climb one of the towers. If you choose this option, you must choose whether to go up the Nativity or the Passion Tower. If you have any accessibility issues, you cannot go up the towers.

Ticket type	Price
General admission	€ 40
Students or visitors under 30 years old	€ 38
Seniors	€ 32
Children under 11 years old	Free

Sagrada Família With Towers

Ticket type	Price
General admission	€ 36
Students or visitors under 30 years old	€ 34
Seniors	€ 28
Children under 11 years old	Free

Barri Gòtic

Barri Gòtic (Gothic Quarter) is the oldest neighborhood in Barcelona, dating back 2,000 years ago to when the Roman Emperor Augustus reigned over the city. There are plenty of streets and alleyways to explore. Among them, you'll find plenty of buildings and structures that date back to the Medieval and Roman eras, many of which are worth exploring:

- **Check out the Carrer del Bisbe bridge on Carrer del Bisbe**: This stunning neo-gothic bridge was designed for the 1929 Barcelona International Exhibition. You'll see why this is one of the most popular spots for tourists to visit, as many love to marvel at its stunning Gothic-style arches and the intricate details of this bridge. Depending on the time of day, the bridge's characteristics change slightly based on the daylight.

- **Look for Roman ruins:** Since the Gothic Quarter dates back to the Roman period, you'll likely find some Roman ruins—if you know where to look. If you go to the Barcelona Cathedral in Placa Nova, you'll find the ruins of a Roman wall. If you venture down Carrer Paradis, you'll see four intact columns from the Temple of Augustus dating back to the first century in a small courtyard.
- **Marval at La Seu Barcelona Cathedral**: Although you'll likely visit the Barcelona Cathedral to look for Roman ruins, this beautiful church is also a must. La Seu Barcelona Cathedral was built between 1298 and 1448 in honor of Santa Eulalia, the patron saint of Barcelona.

Palau de la Música Catalana

Address: Carrer del Palau de la Música, 4-6, 08003 Barcelona

Hours of operation

There are two locations where you can purchase your tickets if you decide to buy them on the day of: At Sant Pere Més Alt, s/n: 8:30 a.m. to 3:30 p.m. and at Palau de la Música, 4-6: 9:30 a.m. to 3:30 p.m.

Regarded as one of Catalan's finest examples of Catalan modernist architecture, you'll be amazed by how beautiful Palau de la Música is—not just on the exterior but also on the interior.

Built in the early 20th century by the famous Catalan architect Lluís Domènech i Montaner, this music hall features many intricate sculptures and colorful mosaics. But aside from its exceptional acoustics, the Palau is the only concert hall with natural light to illuminate it, thanks to its stained-glass ceiling, making this theater stand apart from other traditional concert halls. If there is anything you must see while in Barcelona, it's paying a visit to Palau, whether it's experiencing a show or taking a tour.

Self-Guided Tour

You can book your self-guided tours between 9 a.m. and 3:30 p.m., which should take at most 50 minutes.

Ticket type	Price
General Admission	€ 18
Children under 10 years old	Free

Audio-Guided Tour

Audio-guided tours come with a downloaded audio guide to your phone to enhance your tour. You'll get an in-depth explanation of the images and music that grace this magnificent stage. You can book your audio-guided tour between 9 a.m. and 3:30 p.m., which should take at most 50 minutes.

Ticket type	Price
General Admission	€ 22
Children under 10 years old	Free

Guided Tour

The guided tour option will allow you to go more in-depth with one of the experts at Palau de la Música Catalana. You can book a guided tour between 9 a.m. and 3 p.m., which is around 50 minutes.

Ticket type	Price
General Admission	€ 22
Visitors under 35 years old	€ 18
Seniors 65 years old and up	€ 16
Children under 10 years old	Free

Self-Guided and Guided Tour With a Professional Photo Shoot

If you want to do something unique besides touring Palau de la Música Catalana, add a professional photo shoot to your tour. You'll get a photo session in some of the theater's best spots while exploring and learning about its history. This will include the audio guide if you do a self-guided tour.

The schedule for this option is between 9 a.m. and 12 p.m. (the last time slot for the photo session is at 12:30 p.m.)

Ticket type	Price
General Admission	€ 33
Children under 10 years old	€ 11

Museu Picasso de Barcelona

Address: C/ Montcada, 15-23, 08003 Barcelona

Hours of operation: 10 a.m. to 7 p.m. from Tuesday to Sunday (the last admission is at 6:30 p.m.)

The Museu Picasso de Barcelona (Picasso Museum) is a must-visit destination for art enthusiasts. Founded in 1962, this museum houses an impressive collection of 4,000 Pablo Picasso's art. Throughout the museum, you can expect to see a range of his work, from sketches to paintings, sculptures, and ceramics, all showcasing his evolution as an artist from his earlier years to his more famous pieces.

Guided tours are available and are an additional fee along with your admission:

- Tuesdays at 1 p.m. and 6 p.m.
- Saturdays at 10:15 a.m., 11:30 a.m., and 1 p.m.
- Sundays at 11 a.m., 11:15 a.m., 12:30 p.m., and 12:45 p.m.

Ticket type	Online price	Box office price
General Admission	€ 14	€ 15
Students (18 to 24 years old) and seniors (65 years old and up)	€ 7.50	€ 7.50
Children under 18 years old	Free	Free
Guided tour	€ 6	€ 6

Money-saving tip: If you aren't crunched for time, go to the museum on these days for free access to peruse the collection and temporary exhibitions: Thursdays from 4 p.m. to 7 p.m. and the first Sunday of each month.

If you go during the free hours, you still need a ticket with your selected time slot, which you can book up to four days in advance.

Catedra de la Santa Cruz Y Santa Eulalia

Address: Pla de la Seu, s/n 08002 Barcelona

Hours of operation

- Monday to Friday: 9:30 a.m. to 6:30 p.m. (the last admission is at 5:45 p.m.)
- Saturday and festive vigil: 9:30 a.m. to 5:15 p.m. (the last admission is at 4:30 p.m.)
- Sunday and festive vigil: 2 p.m. to 5 p.m. (the last admission is at 4:30 p.m.)

The Catedra de la Santa Cruz Y Santa Eulalia, also known as the Barcelona Cathedral, is one we touched on with things to explore in Barcelona's Gothic Quarter—but let's go deeper into the significance of this cathedral.

The Catedra de la Santa Cruz Y Santa Eulalia has existed since the 13th century, with the final touches added by the 19th century.

This cathedral is significant to Barcelona for several reasons. First, it houses the Archbishop's throne and, as such, is the seat of the Archbishop of Barcelona.

Second, this cathedral is home to several Gothic paintings created by Guerau Gener, Gabriel Alemany, Bernat Martorell, and Lluis Borrassà. Second, given that this cathedral saw several centuries pass it by, there are many different nods to different periods, including the Chapel of Saint Lucia, built between 1257 and 1296, the Chapter House dating back to the 17th century, and the Chapel of Lepanto dating back to 1407.

One of the most impressive features of the Barcelona Cathedral is the cloister, built between the 14th and 15th centuries. This cloister has four galleries and a tranquil garden in the middle home to geese, palm trees, magnolias, and an orange tree. For a higher perspective, you can take an elevator to the cathedral's rooftop, giving you stunning views of Barcelona and a close-up of the bell towers.

When you visit this cathedral, please remember to dress appropriately because it is a place of worship.

Ticket type	Price
General Admission	€ 14
Children (4 to 12 years old)	€ 6
Children under 3 years old	Free

Bogatell Beach

If you are in Barcelona during the hot summer months, check out Bogatell Beach in the Poblenou neighborhood. This beach was constructed in the early 1990s for the 1992 Summer Olympics and is now famous for beachgoers. Here, you can soak up the sun on the golden sand while enjoying or swimming in the gorgeous blue Mediterranean waters. There are also beach volleyball courts available and free to use.

Check out the neighborhood after you're done lazing about in the sun. Before its transformation for the Olympics, Poblenou was an industrial area with many warehouses. Those buildings have since been transformed into art studios and craft beer breweries worth exploring.

Casa Mila (La Pedrera)

Address: Pg. de Gràcia, 92, L'Eixample, 08008 Barcelona

Hours of operation

- November to February: 9 a.m. to 6:30 p.m. (night tours run from 9 p.m. to 11 p.m.)
- March to October: 9 a.m. to 8:30 p.m. (night tours run from 9 p.m. to 11 p.m.)

Casa Mila has to be one of the most extraordinary buildings in Barcelona, and this picture does not do it justice! Designed by the famous architect Antoni Gaudí, this fantastic building was built between 1906 and 1912 and is considered one of Gaudí's most iconic architectural works. This building is renowned for its curtain wall facade of over 6,000 blocks of stone connected by metal components. The rooftop is also stunning, with sculptured chimneys and panoramic views of Barcelona.

If you visit Casa Mila, you can take a guided tour to explore the building's unique architectural features, including the rooftop terrace, the attic space, the Pedrera

Apartment, the Carrer de Provença courtyards, the main floor, and the Passeig de Gràcia. You can also take advantage of other experiences.

La Pedrera Essential

This option is a self-guided tour, where you can explore the building at your own pace. It also includes a free audio guide to learn more about its history.

Ticket type	Price
General Admission	€ 28
Visitors with a disability (proof must be provided), students, and seniors (65 years old and up)	€ 19
Children (7 to 17 years old)	€ 12.50
Children under 7 years old	Free

La Pedrera Full Experience

The La Pedrera Full Experience is a fully immersive tour with mixed reality glasses and the opportunity to explore exclusive spaces in the building. This experience is not suitable for children under 10.

Ticket type	Price
General Admission	€ 38
Visitors with a disability (proof must be provided), students, and seniors (65 years old and up)	€ 29
Children (7 to 17 years old)	€ 22.50
Children under 7 years old	Free

La Pedrera Night Experience

Take your experience at Casa Mila to the next level and join a guided tour during the La Pedrera Night Experience. You will join one of the experts as they bring you around the building while you enjoy a glass of cava. This experience also includes a show on the rooftop and audio-visual screenings. Please note that this experience is only partially accessible, and you will not see the Pedrera Apartment.

Ticket Type	Price
General Admission	€ 39
Children (7 to 17 years old)	€ 19
Children under seven years old	Free

La Pedrera Premium

Join a small group for a unique tour of Casa Mila. With a tour guide, you'll explore exclusive areas of the building and its main parts. The experience concludes with a private cava tasting in a cozy setting. The tour is limited to six people per group.

Ticket type	Price
General Admission	€ 120
Children under seven years old	Free

La Pedrera Sunrise

I highly recommend this experience, especially if it's your last morning in Barcelona! In this experience, you'll get to explore Casa Mila before others. If you're there early enough (and if it will be sunny), you should be able to catch the sunrise over the city.

Ticket type	Price
General Admission	€ 39
Children (7 to 17 years old)	€ 19.50
Children under seven years old	Free

La Pedrera Essential and Night Experience

This is an excellent combination experience if you want to experience Casa Mila during the day and night. You'll explore the building and its appearance during the day, then return in the evening to experience it at night!

Ticket type	Price
General Admission	€ 39
Children (7 to 17 years old)	€ 22.50
Children under seven years old	Free

What Festivals to Enjoy in Barcelona

Carnestoltes

Carnestoltes, or the Barcelona Carnival, is an annual festival held seven weeks after the first full moon leading up to Ash Wednesday. This festival offers many ways to immerse yourself in Barcelona's culture, including parades, music, and street parties. As this festival leads into Lent, there will be plenty of great eats to try that many will swear off for the 40 days following Ash Wednesday, so be sure to enjoy the sweet and savory treats!

Dia De Sant Jordi

Dia De Sant Jordi (or the Festival of Sant Jordi) is a literature lovers' festival celebrating books and love every year on April 23. This unique festival in Catalonia blends various traditions from different eras. Part of this festival celebrates Sant Jordi, who has been Catalonia's patron saint for centuries. However, it also celebrates the legendary tales of Saint George and the dragon, where he saved the princess and presented her with a red rose from the dragon's body. Additionally, this day is connected to the medieval custom of visiting the Chapel of Sant Jordi to attend a rose fair known as the "lovers' fair." As a result, Sant Jordi is regarded as the patron saint of lovers in Catalonia.

This festival is a great time to explore Barcelona's streets and absorb the energy of the atmosphere. Plenty of stalls are set up where you can look at books and gifts for your significant other. If you want to immerse yourself in this festival further, check out some workshops and recitals centered around literature.

La Mercè

Every September, Barcelona celebrates Mercè, its patron saint. This is a busy festival with several cultural activities for all ages. Some highlights include traditional dances from around Catalonia, a procession of giants and dwarfs, a fire run, and parades. This festival is another excellent way to immerse yourself in Barcelona's traditions and learn more about its heritage.

Where to Eat in Barcelona

In Barcelona, food isn't just about fueling your body so you can keep exploring the city. It's about an experience and celebrating tradition while exploring your taste buds. Here are some of the top places to eat while in Barcelona.

Taps

Address: C/ Mare de Deu del Remei, 53, 08004 Barcelona

Taps is a great place for tapas (and it's budget-friendly, too)! This family-run restaurant has plenty of trim dish options, perfect for sharing, trying something you may never have thought to try before, and gluten-free and vegan options.

Mimo's Born

Address: Placa de Jacint Reventos, 08003 Barcelona, Spain

For another budget-friendly option, check out Mimo's Born. This is another tapas restaurant serving delicious eats to snack on or share with your traveling companion. The sangrias are also delicious here!

Caminito Grill Steak House

Address: Calle de l'Atlantida, 27, 29, 08003 Barcelona Spain

Caminito Grill Steak House is an Argentinean restaurant serving delicious steak and other great dishes. This restaurant is highly rated and budget-friendly, especially if you're stopping in for lunch!

Sensato

Address: Calle Septimània 36, 08006 Barcelona

You don't have to eat Spanish food even if you're in Spain. Sensato is an excellent option for sushi lovers. This restaurant is small, with only eight seats, so it's best to make a reservation to avoid disappointment.

Berbena

Address: Carrer de Minerva, 6, 08006 Barcelona

Although Berbena is a mid-range restaurant, it's also a Michelin star, serving small plates made with in-season ingredients. You can expect a wide variety of shellfish and seafood and plenty of vegetable dishes at Berbena.

What to Eat in Barcelona

Tapas:

Tapas are a quintessential Spanish dining experience, and Barcelona offers an abundance of tapas bars. These small, shareable dishes come in various forms, including patatas bravas (fried potatoes with spicy tomato sauce), gambas al ajillo (garlic shrimp), and chorizo al vino (chorizo cooked in red wine).

Paella:

Originating from Valencia, paella is a Spanish rice dish that has become popular throughout the country. In Barcelona, you can find various versions of paella, featuring a mix of rice, saffron, vegetables, and a variety of proteins like chicken, rabbit, or seafood.

Crema Catalana:

Crema Catalana is a traditional Catalan dessert similar to crème brûlée. It consists of a creamy custard base with a layer of caramelized sugar on top. The subtle flavors of vanilla and citrus make it a delightful way to end a meal.

Escudella i Carn d'Olla:

This traditional Catalan dish is often enjoyed during the winter holidays. Escudella i Carn d'Olla is a hearty stew that includes a variety of meats, such as sausage and pork, along with vegetables. The broth is later used to cook rice or pasta.

Cava:

While not a dish, Cava is a sparkling wine that is synonymous with celebrations in Catalonia. Barcelona and the surrounding Penedès region are known for their production of Cava. Enjoy a glass of this bubbly wine to complement your meal or toast to a memorable trip.

Where to Stay in Barcelona

With so many great places to explore in Barcelona, you'll wonder where you should stay. These options are some top picks with high ratings! All you need to decide is what neighborhood you want to stay in.

Praktik Garden

Address: Diputació, 325, Eixample, 08009 Barcelona

If you have never been to Barcelona, you may want to choose an accommodation central to most attractions. The Praktik Garden is a two-star hotel near several attractions and public transportation. If you can, choose a room with a balcony to enjoy some fresh evening air after a day of exploring.

Hotel 1898

Address: La Rambla, 109, Ciutat Vella, 08002 Barcelona

Hotel 1898 is an upscale accommodation in the heart of Barcelona. The rates are slightly higher, but the interior is stunning, with spacious rooms, a heated rooftop pool, and spa services. This hotel is also a short distance from Barcelona's Gothic Quarter, allowing you to be close to plenty of areas to explore in this part of the city.

Be Mate Paseo de Gracia

Address: Passeig de Gràcia, 115, Gràcia, 08008 Barcelona

Be Mate Paseo de Gracia offers spacious, apartment-sized rooms with kitchenettes for self-catering. Some apartments overlook a beautiful garden terrace. The accommodation is within walking distance of some of Barcelona's attractions and Tivoli Theater.

Hotel Arts

Address: Marina, 19-21, 08005 Barcelona

Hotel Arts is a great place to stay if you want a luxury hotel near the beach and Barcelona's city center. The hotel is next to the beach, giving you stunning views of the Mediterranean Sea and Barcelona. The rooms are spacious and comfortable. Hotel Arts also has a spa, fashion boutiques, and five restaurants.

Sant Jordi Hostels Rock Palace

Address: Balmes, 75, Eixample, 08007 Barcelona

Sant Jordi Hostels Rock Palace is a great hostel for music lovers who want fun, themed accommodation at an affordable rate. This hostel is five minutes from the Passeig de Gràcia Metro Station for your convenience and has a rooftop terrace and an outdoor pool. If you're backpacking, this place also has laundry you can use for a small fee.

Hotel Ginebra

Address: Rambla de Catalunya 1, Eixample, 08007 Barcelona

Hotel Ginebra is a budget-friendly option in a 19th-century Gothic building with a stunning interior and modern rooms. This hotel is within walking distance of Barcelona's Gothic Quarter, public transportation, and the luxury boutiques on Paseo de Gracia. A range of room options is available, including rooms with city views or a balcony.

Barcelona Hotel Colonial

Address: Via Laietana, 3, Ciutat Vella, 08003 Barcelona

Barcelona Hotel Colonial is a beautiful hotel set in a stone building with a clock tower. This hotel is in the heart of Barcelona's Gothic Quarter and features comfortable, spacious rooms with wood flooring, a minibar, and the necessary amenities.

Hotel Ronda Lesseps

Address: Ballester, 77-81, Gràcia, 08023 Barcelona

Hotel Ronda Lesseps is another mid-range option in the Gràcia neighborhood. It offers several room options, including family rooms, all of which are bright and comfortable. In addition, this accommodation has two garden terraces where you can relax after a day of exploring Barcelona.

Barceloneta Suites Apartments Beach

Address: Carrer de Grau i Torras, 17, Ciutat Vella, 08003 Barcelona

For another self-catering option within walking distance of Barcelona's beaches, check out Barceloneta Suites Apartments Beach. These budget-friendly apartments are also within walking distance of the Picasso Museum. All units feature a coffee machine, toaster, and fridge; some rooms have a balcony or views of the Mediterranean Sea.

Acevi Villarroel

Address: Calle Villarroel 106, 08011 Barcelona

Acevi Villarroel is a mid-range option offering simple yet elegant rooms. Staying at this hotel will put you within walking distance of Barcelona's attractions. They also have a rooftop terrace and pool to enjoy, as well as a spa for an extra charge.

What Not to Do in Barcelona

Here are some good things to keep in mind when you're planning your trip to Barcelona.

Don't Stay Outside the City Center

Staying outside the city center may feel tempting, especially for budget purposes. However, staying further out from the city center will remove you from many of Barcelona's attractions and local festivities, especially with Barcelona being as vibrant as it is. You'll spend more time trying to travel rather than being as close to the action as possible, so try to stick to staying in accommodations close to Barcelona's city center.

Don't Expect Barcelona to Be Warm Year Round

Yes, Barcelona has plenty of beaches to enjoy if that's one of the main reasons you want to visit this city. However, while it may seem like a tropical paradise, it's not warm all year round. Barcelona is quite chilly between December and February. So, while you may be unable to hang out at the beach during these months, don't let it deter you from exploring the rest of the city. Grab some Spanish hot chocolate and meander the beautiful streets.

Don't Wear High Heels

High heels may be tempting, but Barcelona has plenty of cobblestone streets that need to match better with high heels. Opt to wear comfortable flats or sneakers to save yourself a potential injury.

Don't Go to These Neighborhoods

Barcelona is safe, but there are a few shady neighborhoods to avoid, especially at night. They are El Raval, Besòs, and La Mina.

Beware of Jellyfish on Bogatell Beach

Keep an eye out for jellyfish on Bogatell Beach, especially during warmer months when they may be more prevalent. Avoid swimming near jellyfish or touching them, as their stings can be painful and potentially dangerous.

Don't Forget to Visit the Roof Terrace of Casa Mila

The Roof Terrace of Casa Milà is one of its most iconic features, with its unique chimneys and panoramic views of Barcelona. Avoid skipping the Roof Terrace, as it offers a memorable experience and fantastic photo opportunities.

Don't forget to use the Audio Guide at Casa Mila

Audio guides are available in multiple languages and offer detailed commentary as you explore Casa Milà. Avoid missing out on valuable information by not using audio guides, which can enhance your understanding and appreciation of the building's architecture and history.

Next Stop: A Coruña

One of the fantastic things about Barcelona is that it is a masterpiece of history, culture, and life. Its rich heritage, stunning architecture, and vibrant atmosphere make visiting this city a must for travelers worldwide. No matter what you decide, you'll find ways to immerse yourself entirely in its culture and way of life.

The next chapter will explore A Coruña, a hidden gem on Spain's northwest coast. This beautiful area is a great spot to visit during summer, thanks to its gorgeous beaches. However, there are plenty of historical sites and festivals to immerse yourself in!

Chapter 5:

A Coruña —Dos and Don'ts

R emember earlier in the book how I mentioned Spain is full of many different languages? In A Coruña, Spanish is widely spoken and understood. However, the Galician language is A Coruña's local language. Here are some quick phrases to learn:

- **Hello** : Ola
- **How are you?:** Como estás?
- **How do I get to...:** Como chego...
- **Thank you:** Grazas

Some of these phrases are similar to, if not mirror, the typical Spanish language. But can you spot some of the differences?

Discovering A Coruña

A Coruña, also known as La Coruña, is a stunning coastal city in northwest Spain with a vast oceanfront. This vibrant region dates back to the Roman era and played a significant role in the Spanish Armada's departure in 1588 when the Spaniards went to invade England.

A Coruña has many beautiful beaches. However, the Riazor is the most popular for surfers. This coastal town has many famous landmarks to explore, from the Tower of Hercules (Torre de Hércules) to the commemorative Obelisco. There are many things to see, do, enjoy, and eat, so let's get right into what to do in A Coruña!

What to Do in A Coruña

Torre de Hércules

Address: Avenida Navarra, s/n, 15002 A Coruña

Hours of operation: 10 a.m. to 4 p.m. daily

The Torre de Hércules is an impressive ancient lighthouse dating back to Roman times. Named after the famous god from Greek and Roman mythology, this impressive tower is the oldest working lighthouse in the world and has been in operation for nearly 2,000 years! As it has been around and working for this long, it is one of A Coruña's most important landmarks and is a UNESCO World Heritage Site.

This tower is a beautiful landmark and a symbol of A Coruña's rich history and cultural heritage. This beautiful lighthouse is a testament to the ingenuity and skill of the ancient Romans who built it and is a reminder of the importance of preserving these cultural treasures. When you visit the Torre de Hércules, take in as much history as you can from the visitor center, then climb to the top to see the surrounding coastline from way up in the sky while admiring the brilliant architecture.

Ticket type	Price
General Admission	€ 3.09
Youth (16 years old and under) and seniors (65 years old and up)	€ 1.55
Children under three or visitors with a disability (proof must be provided)	Free

Castillo de San Antón

Address: P.º Marítimo Alcalde Francisco Vázquez, 2, 15001 A Coruña

Hours of operation

- Tuesday to Saturday: 10 a.m. to 7:40 p.m.
- Sunday: 10 a.m. to 2:30 p.m.
- Closed on Mondays

Castillo de San Antón is one of the fortresses on your must-visit bucket list while in A Coruña. Dating back to the 16th century and named after Saint Anthony of Padua, the city's patron saint, Catillo de San Antón was built to protect the city from attacks by invaders coming in by sea. It later became a prison, then a place to quarantine ill soldiers.

Today, the castle houses the Archaeological and Historical Museum of A Coruña, which has an exciting display of archaeological artifacts, paintings, and other exhibits that display A Coruña's history from its earlier years to the present. Additionally, as Castillo de San Antón was a fortress, you can explore the castle's interior and climb the towers to take panoramic views of A Coruña.

Ticket type	Price
General Admission	€ 3.06
Youth (14 years old and under) and seniors (65 years old and up)	€ 1.03

Monte de San Pedro

Address: Av Fernando Suárez García, 15011 A Coruña

Monte de San Pedro is A Coruña's best secret. This stunning national park overlooks the Atlantic Ocean, offering a beautiful, lush green space to enjoy the fresh A Coruña air. Several walking trails wind through the park, and there is a maze for you to explore. For history buffs, there is a military installation with two large guns from the 1920s you can check out, too. Additionally, many tourists love visiting Monte de San Pedro in the evening to watch the sunset.

Plaza de María Pita

The Plaza de María Pita is in the heart of A Coruña and is a dedication to the heroine of the same name who helped to defend the city against an English invasion during the 16th century. This square has many iconic buildings, including City Hall, the Palace of the Captaincy, the Church of St. George (Iglesia de San Jorge), and a statue of María Pita. This square is a great spot to stroll through and take in the architecture leisurely. Events and festivals are also held here depending on the time of year.

Menhires Pola Paz

Address: Paseo dos Menhires, 15002 A Coruña

Menhires Pola Paz is a beautiful set of 10 upright stones overlooking the Atlantic Ocean, created by sculptor Manolo Paz. These menhirs, also called the Family of Menhirs or Menhirs of Peace, have holes carved into them, allowing visitors to look through and make their interpretations. Paz intended for visitors to reflect on their future and what it holds.

This is a popular area, not just for the sculpture park but also for the stunning views of the Atlantic Ocean. Even if people aren't coming here for reflection, people love it for its tranquility. It also looks stunning at night!

Plaza del Humor

The Plaza del Humor is precisely what it sounds like a square filled with humor. This square has plenty of well-known characters that have made us laugh, including the Pink Panther and Cervantes. Be sure to take lots of photos here, as there will be plenty of opportunities!

What Festivals to Enjoy in A Coruña

Festival of San Juan

Check out the Festival of San Juan if you plan to visit Spain in June. This ancient festival is one of A Coruña's most significant celebrations as it marks the start of summer. At this festival, you can enjoy bonfires, fireworks, music, dancing, and great food—grilled sardines are a specialty for this occasion!

Festivals of María Pita

The festivals of María Pit in A Coruña celebrate the legendary heroine who defended the city during a British attack led by Sir Francis Drake in 1589. Held in mid-August, the festival honors this important Spanish figure and includes parades, music, fireworks, and other cultural events.

Mozart Festival

Classical music enthusiasts looking to immerse themselves in a classical music festival should watch the Mozart Festival. It is unclear why he is significant in Spain, but A Coruña holds a festival every May and June to honor the great musician and composer. In addition to the orchestra playing several of his musical pieces, you'll also hear other pieces from the Baroque period and the Italian Rossini. This will make for a lovely night out while in A Coruña.

Where to Eat in A Coruña

Since A Coruña is right along the Atlantic Ocean, its food scene is famous for its delicious seafood. Many of A Coruña's restaurants offer a variety of fresh fish and shellfish dishes, including octopus, clams, and sardines. The signature dish of this region is the pulpo a la gallega (Galician-style octopus), and it is a must-try for seafood lovers. If seafood isn't your fancy, don't worry! A Coruña is famous for its empanadas (savory pies), Padron peppers, and Albariño wine.

A Mundiña

Address: Rúa Real, 77, 15003 A Coruña

A Mudiña has been around A Coruña since 2006, serving traditional Galician dishes. This restaurant is renowned for its ethical practices in making seafood dishes, so you can expect the best quality delivered to your table!

Deabejas

Address: Calle de los Olmos 2, 15003 A Coruña

The charming Deabejas restaurant is located in the heart of A Coruña. This budget-friendly establishment offers tapas to suit anyone's taste buds, complete with sangria. Its dessert selection is also a popular choice among visitors.

Pulpeira de Lola la Antigua de Melide

Address: Ronda do Outeiro 135, 15007 A Coruña

Pulpeira de Lola la Antigua de Melide is another excellent tapas restaurant serving plenty of Galecian-style dishes. This restaurant has been highly praised for its pulpo, cecina (meat carpaccio), and mejillones (mussels). It's best to book a reservation here if you want to check it out, as this restaurant is quite busy and popular.

Pablo Gallego

Address: Calle Capitan Troncoso, 4, 15001 A Coruña

Pablo Gallego is another popular option among locals and travelers. The restaurant is named after its owner and head chef, Pablo Gallego Lodeiro, who is known for creating delicious Galician-style meals. The cozy atmosphere of Pablo Gallego and the yummy foods satisfy any cravings, especially if you want to try squid, octopus, or crab.

EME Taberna Contemporanea

Address: Rúa Magistrado Manuel Artime, 21, bajo, 15004 A Coruña

At EME Taberna Contemporanea, you'll have your choice of many dishes, some that follow traditional Galician styles and others that are innovative. In addition to a menu that will please anyone's taste buds, you'll find a great selection of wine and other drinks to enjoy with your meal.

What to Eat in A Coruña

Galician-Style Octopus

Pulpo a la Gallega is a quintessential Galician dish. It features an octopus that is cooked until tender, sliced, and then drizzled with olive oil, sprinkled with paprika, and served on a bed of boiled potatoes. The combination of flavors and textures makes it a must-try.

Empanada Gallega

Empanada Gallega is a savory pie filled with a variety of ingredients, such as tuna, peppers, onions, and sometimes hard-boiled eggs. The crust is typically made with a dough that can be either flaky or bread-like. Empanadas are a popular snack or meal option in A Coruña.

Percebes

Percebes are a delicacy in Galicia, and A Coruña is a great place to try them. These unique seafood delicacies resemble small dinosaur claws and are known for their briny flavor. They are often enjoyed simply boiled and served with a side of lemon.

Zorza

Zorza is a traditional Galician dish made with marinated and seasoned pork, typically pork shoulder or loin. The meat is seasoned with paprika, garlic, and other spices, then grilled or fried. It's a flavorful and hearty dish that showcases Galicia's love for pork.

Tarta de Santiago

Tarta de Santiago is a popular dessert named after the patron saint of Spain, Saint James. It's an almond cake topped with the cross of Saint James, made from powdered sugar. This delicious cake is often enjoyed with a cup of coffee or a glass of sweet wine.

Where to Stay in A Coruña

Noa Boutique Hotel

Address: Rúa Concepción Arenal, 51, 15179 Santa Cruz, A Coruña

Noa Boutique is a great place to stay if you're seeking a mid-range hotel that overlooks the ocean. This comfortable hotel has floor-to-ceiling windows, modern furnishings, and a rooftop terrace with a hot tub. This hotel is a little outside A Coruña's city center, making it a great spot to return to after a few day trips.

Hesperia Finisterre

Address: Pr. Parrote, 2-4, 15001 A Coruña

If you're looking for a more upscale stay in A Coruña, book your stay at Hesperia Finisterre. This hotel is near the Old Town neighborhood and is a short walk from the harbor, which makes it great for exploring A Coruña on foot. In addition to rooms that overlook the ocean, family rooms are available. This hotel also offers bicycles for hire, a tennis court, and three swimming pools.

Hotel Lois

Address: Rua Estrella 40, 15003 A Coruña

Hotel Lois is a great, budget-friendly option. It is five minutes from the beach and within walking distance of other areas and landmarks to visit while in A Coruña.

Every room is fitted with wooden floors, and some have a balcony overlooking the city. There is also a delicious restaurant on the main floor serving Galician cuisine.

Hotel Mar del Plata

Address: Paseo Rda., 58, 15011 A Coruña

The Hotel Mar del Plata is perfect if you want a romantic stay while exploring A Coruña without breaking the bank. These simple rooms are fitted with rainfall showers, comfortable beds, and great room options that can overlook the ocean or the city. If you want to upgrade, there are rooms with an intimate nook and a freestanding bathtub. They also serve breakfast in the mornings for a small fee.

Eurostars Ciudad de la Coruña

Address: Rúa Juan Sebastián Elcano, 13, 15002 A Coruña

Eurostars is positioned perfectly if you want to be close to the ocean and listen to the waves crashing into the peninsula! This hotel has excellent ocean views with bright and spacious rooms fitted with wooden floors. Some rooms are suites with a separate seating area and a balcony. There are also family room options available.

Exe Coruña

Address: Rúa Ramón y Cajal, 53, 15006 A Coruña

Exe Coruña isn't precisely in the heart of A Coruña's actions, but it is near public transportation, so anything you want to visit isn't a long journey. At this hotel, you will find modern-fitted rooms, bright with splashes of color. This hotel also has great prices that won't break the bank, and breakfast is included with your room fee.

Hotel Plaza Coruña

Address: Rúa Santiago Rey Fernández Latorre, 45, 15006 A Coruña

Luxury stays are always a fun option, especially in A Coruña! Surprisingly, the Hotel Plaza has some days that are cheaper to stay if you're worried about breaking your budget. This hotel's rooms are fitted with contemporary-chic furniture, just as stunning as their rooftop terrace, SkyBar. This hotel is near public transportation to take you to the places you want to see seamlessly, as well as plenty of shops.

Hotel Riazor

Address: Avenida de Pedro Barrié de la Maza, 29, 15004 A Coruña

If you want something closer to A Coruña's Riazor Beach, check out Hotel Riazor. This beautiful hotel boasts bright, neutral-colored rooms and wooden floors; most rooms overlook the ocean! Prices aren't bad, either. They're about mid-range, regardless of the time of year you go.

Eurostars Atlantico

Address: Avenida do Porto da Coruña 4, Oza, 15006 La Coruna

Eurostars Atlantico is in a perfect spot if you're looking to check out great dining options and be close to nearby attractions. The rooms are gorgeous, bright, and spacious for relaxing in after spending the day exploring.

Melia Maria Pita

Address: Avenida Pedro Barrié de la Maza, 3, 15003 A Coruña

Melia Maria Pita is next to Orzán Beach, offering stunning, bright rooms with beautiful ocean views! Your rooms will come with crisp sheets, a minibar, a desk, and a satellite TV. This hotel also has a great restaurant that can accommodate those who need to follow a gluten-free diet.

What Not to Do in A Coruña

A Coruña has plenty of things to see and do. However, as it is a coastal city that can become busy, keep these tips in mind to ensure a great trip in this region of Spain!

Don't Forget to Check Weather alerts

A Coruña's weather can be unpredictable, with rain common throughout the year. Avoid being caught unprepared by checking the weather forecast before your visit and bringing appropriate clothing, including a waterproof jacket or umbrella.

Don't Drink the Tap Water

Given that A Coruña is near the ocean, the tap water may contain higher than average mineral content, which can upset your stomach or make you ill. While in A Coruña, you're better off drinking bottled water to avoid getting sick.

Don't Drive in the City Center

A Coruña's city center can be challenging due to the narrow streets and heavy traffic (especially in the summer). In addition, many roads are one-way, so getting lost or turned around can be easy when figuring out where to go. Opt for public transportation or walking instead. Besides, you'll be able to see more without the stress of trying to get around!

Don't Swim During Red Flag Warnings

While you may intend to spend at least a day at one of A Coruña's beaches, if you see a red flag posted, you shouldn't swim in the water due to dangerous sea conditions. This warning is posted if strong currents, high waves, or other factors make it unsafe for people to swim.

Don't Miss Climbing on the Top of Torre de Hércules

The Torre de Hércules offers stunning panoramic views of the Atlantic Ocean and the city of La Coruña from its summit. Avoid missing the opportunity to climb to the top of the tower and enjoy the breathtaking views.

Don't Rush visiting Monte de Pedro

Monte de San Pedro is a peaceful and scenic retreat from the hustle and bustle of the city. Avoid rushing through your visit and take time to relax, enjoy the views, and appreciate the natural beauty of the park.

Next Stop: Salamanca

A Coruña's rich history and beautiful landscape offer many ways to appreciate its natural beauty. From exploring the ancient Tower of Hercules to reflecting on your life as you peer through the holes in the Menhires Pola Paz's stones, this city will surely leave you feeling inspired by its rich heritage.

In the next chapter, we will explore Salamanca, a stunning city home to the oldest University in Europe, the Universidad de Salamanca. This city has much to see and do, so let's start planning!

Chapter 6:

Salamanca—Dos and Don'ts

SPAIN

There are plenty of beautiful places in the world, but nothing like Spain's Salamanca! Salamanca is also called La Dorada, "the golden one." The city's many sandstone buildings glow when the sun sets, and the streetlights turn on.

Discovering Salamanca

Salamanca's history dates back to the third century when the Carthaginians first inhabited the city. Then, the Romans settled in until the Moors took over in the 11th century. Of course, the city has seen several evolutions over the centuries since then, and there is plenty to explore while there.

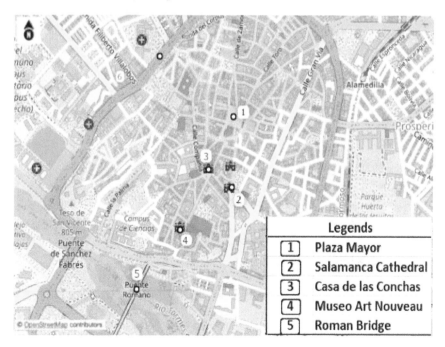

Legends

1	Plaza Mayor
2	Salamanca Cathedral
3	Casa de las Conchas
4	Museo Art Nouveau
5	Roman Bridge

Given how far back Salamanca's history goes, it is also home to the oldest university in Europe. You'll find plenty of historical pieces in this city throughout the streets. The most noteworthy landmarks include the Plaza Mayor, the Roman Bridge, and the Cathedral Nueva.

What to Do in Salamanca

Visiting Salamanca will bring you back in time. It's one of the most beautiful Spanish cities, primarily because it houses Europe's oldest universities. As you explore Salamanca, you will quickly understand why the city's heart has been listed as a UNESCO World Heritage site. Let's explore some of the things to do in Salamanca.

Plaza Mayor

Plaza Mayor is Salamanca's central square, which dates back to the 18th century. Alberto Churriguera designed this beautiful square and its surrounding buildings between 1729 and 1755, displaying the fine work of the Baroque period. Around the square, you'll also see plenty of medallions representing important Spanish figures, including Cervantes, St. Theresa, Ferdinand VI, Charles I, and Alfonso XI.

During the day, this place is a beautiful spot to enjoy some drinks or meals at one of the restaurants. You may even want to grab a coffee and sit outside to people-watch and take in the beautiful sights of the square. It's also a good idea to come back in the evening as it looks stunning with the city lights illuminating the buildings.

The Old and New Cathedrals of Salamanca

Address: 20 Calle Patio Chico, 37008 Salamanca

Hours of operation

* April to September: 10 a.m. to 8 p.m. (the last entry is at 7:15 p.m.)
* October to March: 10 a.m. to 6 p.m. (the last entry is at 5:15 p.m.)

Salamanca has two cathedrals that sit side by side and are interconnected—so you can visit both with one ticket! The New Cathedral (Catedral Nueva) is the most famous of the two cathedrals, dating back to the 16th century when construction began in 1513. It took over 200 years to complete, so you'll see a mix of styles within the cathedral's interior: Gothic, Renaissance, and Baroque.

On the other hand, the Old Cathedral (Catedral Vieja de Santa María de la Sede) was built in the 12th century and features a mix of Gothic and Romanesque styles. As you walk through this part of the two cathedrals, be sure to explore the apse that depicts the lives of Jesus and the Virgin Mary.

These cathedrals are a rarity in Spain because they are connected. Remember that these are places of worship, so you must be dressed appropriately if you visit.

Ticket type	Price
General Admission	€ 10
Seniors 65 and up	€ 9
Children (7 to 16 years old)	€ 7
Children 6 and under	Free

Casa de las Conchas

Address: C. de la Compañía, 2, 37002 Salamanca

Casa de las Conchas (the House of Shells) is a stunning building dating back to the 15th century. While the house's façade is another excellent display of late Gothic and Plateresque styles, this historical gem has over 300 scallop shells on its exterior. The shells symbolize the journey of pilgrims along the Camino de Santiago Compostela.

The house was a residence for a long time, but in the 1960s, it was also the main building of Menendez Pelayo College. Today, it is the city's public library and information center. It's worth visiting because a courtyard with beautiful gargoyles along the roof crest is in the center.

Old Town

One of the nice things about Salamanca is how small it is. How long you decide to stay is up to you. However, if you only have 24 hours, checking out Old Town should be on your must-visit list.

Salamanca's old town has plenty of character and history in every corner. From the Plaza Mayor to the Casa de las Conchas, there are many things to see, do, and experience from the outside. You should also make it a point to visit the University of Salamanca and take in its beautiful architecture and library. Grab a coffee and allow yourself to get lost in the city.

Museo Art Nouveau and Art Déco de Casa Lis

Address: Calle de Gibraltar, 14, 37008 Salamanca
Hours of operation: 11 a.m. to 8 p.m. daily

The Museo Art Nouveau and Art Déco Casa de Lis are must-visits, especially for art and antique enthusiasts. This museum, built by Miguel de Lis in 1905, houses some of Spain's most important Art Deco and Art Nouveau collections. As you explore this museum, you'll see many sculptures, 19th-century ceramic dolls, antique furniture, paintings, and jewelry.

Ticket type	Price
Adults	€ 5
Students	€ 3
Children (14 years old and under)	Free

Budget-saving tip: If you're in Salamanca on a Thursday, visit the museum between 11 a.m. and 2 p.m., when entry is free.

The Salamanca Roman Bridge

The Salamanca Roman Bridge (Puente Romano de Salamanca) connects the banks of Salamanca over the Tormes River. This picturesque bridge dates back to the first century, but much of the bridge standing today was rebuilt in the 18th century. If you want to admire some of the work from the Roman era, 15 of the 26 arches remain.

Visiting this bridge is a great starting point for immersing yourself in Salamanca's architecture. The river flowing below the bridge also provides a scenic backdrop.

What Festivals to Enjoy in Salamanca

Los Reyes Magos

Christmas might come and go around the world in the blink of an eye, but Spain has another holiday celebration they enjoy: Los Reyes Magos.

Los Reyes Magos, or the three wise men, are based on the famous biblical tale of the three men who journeyed to Bethlehem to welcome Jesus. This holiday happens on January 6. On the eve of Los Reyes Magos, many cities will gather in the streets to watch a parade, similar to seeing a Santa Claus parade in North America. Attending these events is a great way to immerse yourself in Spanish heritage and get a feel for their holiday magic.

El Carnaval del Toro

El Carnaval del Toro is a famous festival celebrated annually in Ciudad Rodrigo, a small town just an hour by car from Salamanca. This festival, known as the "Bull Carnival," involves bullfighting and other traditional activities. The highlight of this festival is the horse bull run. However, there is also carnival dancing, amateur bullfights, and plenty of live music to enjoy.

San Juan de Sahagún

San Juan de Sahagún is a big celebration in Salamanca's Plaza de los Bandos. This critical and celebrated figure in Spanish history helped to mitigate a confrontation between two of Salamanca's noble families in the 15th century. He is also praised as a hero who saved a boy who fell into a well and tamed a bull that had been terrorizing the city.

The city celebrates San Juan every June 12, and at this celebration, you can take in more of Spain's heritage and enjoy fireworks in the evening. Tons of entertainment take place for you to enjoy, too.

Corpus Christi

Corpus Christi is a religious celebration in Spain that takes place nine weeks after Easter on a Thursday after the Holiday Trinity Sunday. Many cities have their way of celebrating this holiday. However, Salamanca celebrates Corpus Christi by combining a procession of the saint and the moss men.

In addition to the parade, you can immerse yourself in the celebrations by attending plays and exhibitions in the city. It's also a great idea to walk around and admire the colorful balconies decorated for the occasion.

Fiesta de Santiago Apóstol

The Fiesta de Santiago Apóstol celebrates Spain's patron saint. This national holiday takes place on July 25 and includes fireworks and traditional dances. However, if you're in Salamanca on that date, you may see bullfights and other street party fun!

Where to Eat in Salamanca

Salamanca's food scene is best known for its mix of traditional Spanish dishes and local specialties. Additionally, Salamanca is famous for its cured meats and pork-based dishes. This is a great place to eat if you're a bonafide foodie!

La Hoja 21

Address: Calle San Pablo, 21, 37002 Salamanca

Opened in 1998, La Hoja 21 offers a contemporary take on Spanish tapas, focusing on including fresh ingredients from local suppliers. The menu is never the same.

They change it often based on the seasonality of the produce and are always looking to be innovative with the dishes they create for their menus. They also have a prix fixe menu option for lunch and dinner (between €22 and €24). Otherwise, you can expect prices for the individual items to be about mid-range overall.

El Alquimista

Address: Pl. de San Cristóbal, 6, 37001 Salamanca

El Alquimista offers a fusion of Spanish and international cuisine using high-quality ingredients paired with a creative presentation. The food is delicious here, and the staff are warm and welcoming, providing world-class service as you enjoy your meal.

La Pepita Burger Bar

Address: Pl. Ángel, 2, 37001 Salamanca

Looking for a delicious burger? Check out La Pepita Burger Bar. This restaurant is well-loved for its juicy burgers, made with high-quality ingredients. There are plenty of burger options available, regardless of your dietary needs. Additionally, La Pepita Burger has salads, fries, and other starters you can add to your meal.

Diabluras Gastrobar

Address: C. Asaderia, 4, 37001 Salamanca

If you're looking for a great place for tapas, the Diabluras Gastrobar is another excellent option to check out in Salamanca. This restaurant offers delicious options for vegetarians, vegans, and others and traditional Spanish cuisine.

Bar La Viga

Address: C. Consuelo, 14, 37001 Salamanca

Bar La Viga offers affordable menu items that pair well with a beer or sangria. Some popular options are steak tartare, fried calamari, and pork cheek.

What to Eat in Salamanca

Hornazo

Hornazo is a savory pastry filled with a mixture of meats, typically chorizo, bacon, and sometimes pork loin, all encased in a flaky pastry crust. It is often enjoyed during special occasions, festivals, or as a picnic snack.

Iberian Ham

Spain is renowned for its cured hams, and Salamanca is no exception. Try Jamon Iberico, a high-quality cured ham from the Iberian Peninsula. It's often served thinly sliced and can be enjoyed on its own or as part of a charcuterie board.

Alubias de la Granja

Alubias de la Granja are white beans cultivated in the nearby town of La Granja. These beans are often cooked in a flavorful stew with chorizo, blood sausage, and other meats. It's a hearty and delicious dish that showcases the regional ingredients.

Farinato

Farinato is a traditional sausage from Salamanca made with pork, bread crumbs, and a variety of spices. It has a distinctive flavor and is often grilled or fried. Farinato can be served as a tapa or as part of a larger meal.

Cocido Charro

Cocido Charro is a hearty and flavorful stew that is a specialty of the region. It typically includes a variety of meats such as chorizo, morcilla (blood sausage), pork, and vegetables like chickpeas and potatoes. This comforting dish is a true taste of Castilian cuisine.

Where to Stay in Salamanca

Although Salamanca is steeped in history, it's also lively because it is a university city. There are plenty of options you can check out for accommodations. All you need to decide is whether to stay in the city's heart or outside.

Hotel Rector

Address: P.º del Rector Esperabé, 10, 37008 Salamanca

Hotel Rector is a small hotel with only 14 rooms. The interior is cozy in a beautiful stone building, with cream and gold furnishings in the lobby and the rooms. You can choose room sizes from a double to a family room and a deluxe suite. This hotel is within walking distance of several attractions as well.

Grand Hotel Don Gregorio

Address: C. San Pablo, 80, 37008 Salamanca

If you're seeking a more sophisticated type of accommodation, the Grand Hotel Don Gregorio has everything you'd be looking for to suit this need. This hotel has stunning wooden floors in the rooms, a spa, and a gourmet restaurant. Grand Hotel Don Gregorio is within walking distance of both cathedrals, the Plaza Mayor, and designer shopping.

Hacienda Zorita Wine Hotel and Spa

Address: SA-300, km 10, 37115 Valverdón, Salamanca

Set just outside Salamanca's city center in the heart of Duero Valley, the Hacienda Zorita Wine Hotel and Spa was once a monastery dating back 700 years. Although it's been transformed into the beautiful hotel it is today, and its interior still features exposed wooden beams and golden rooms.

This hotel is excellent if you intend to try wines in Spain, as they offer a wide selection produced on the estate. There are also fantastic swimming pools, an open-air cinema, a spa, and a Michelin-star restaurant to enjoy in the summer.

Castillo del Buen Amor

Address: Inca Villanueva de Cañedo Ctra. N-630, Km.317,6, 37799 Topas, Salamanca

Have you ever wanted to stay in a castle? Castillo del Buen Amor is set in an old castle dating back to the 15th century. This beautiful castle has been restored to make you feel like royalty when you stay here. Some of the great features of this accommodation include rooms overlooking the courtyard and countryside, a seasonal outdoor pool, and a library. If you stay at this location, eat in the restaurant at least once. It's in the former dungeons of the castle.

NH Collection Salamanca Palacio de Castellanos

Address: C. San Pablo, 58-64, 37008 Salamanca

If you want to stay in an older part of Salamanca, check out NH Salamanca Palacio de Castellanos Hotel. This hotel is next to the Plaza Mayor. Still, it is also within walking distance of several other parts of the city, including the Plaza de Concilio de Trento, the cathedrals, St. Stephen's Covenant, and the Museum of Art Nouveau and Art Deco Casa Lis.

Salamanca Suite Studios

Address: Plaza Libertad 4, 37002 Salamanca

For a budget-friendly option, check out the Salamanca Suite Studios. This accommodation offers comfortable rooms with a kitchenette, including a microwave, fridge, and kitchen utensils. It is within walking distance of several attractions covered in this chapter.

Catalonia Plaza Mayor

Address: Calle Espoz y Mina 23-25, 37002 Salamanca

The Catalonia Plaza Mayor is a mid-range hotel near the Plaza Mayor. It has 67 rooms, including family rooms, fitted with modern furnishings.

Hotel Alameda Palace

Address: Paseo de La Estación 1 Plaza de España, 37004 Salamanca

The Hotel Alameda Palace is another mid-range hotel option with plenty of things to enjoy while you stay here, including a rooftop pool and a minibar in your room after a day of exploring. This hotel is within walking distance of many of Salamanca's landmarks and restaurants.

Sercotel Las Torres Salamanca

Address: Calle Concejo 4, 37002 Salamanca

Sercotel Las Torres Salamanca is located in the Plaza Mayor, putting you central to all the city's action. This accommodation is set in a beautiful baroque building overlooking the Plaza. Many of the rooms have balconies where you can enjoy city views.

Abba Fonseca Hotel

Address: Plaza San Blas 2, 37007 Salamanca

The Abba Fonseca Hotel offers bright rooms with stunning city and cathedral views. This accommodation has an on-site gym, a small spa with a hot tub and sauna, and a delicious restaurant. There are several room options available, including family-sized rooms.

What Not to Do in Salamanca

Don't Sunbathe in the Plaza Mayor

If there is one thing that locals hate the most, it's people who sunbathe in Salamanca's largest plazas. Stretch out and people-watch while enjoying a snack and some drinks, but don't treat it like the beach!

Avoid Restaurants near Plaza Mayor

Restaurants and cafes in Plaza Mayor may cater primarily to tourists and may have higher prices compared to those in other parts of the city. Avoid overpaying for meals by checking menu prices before sitting down to eat, or consider exploring nearby streets for more affordable options.

Check Restroom Facilities near Plaza Mayor

Restroom facilities may not be readily available in Plaza Mayor itself, especially if you're not dining at one of the restaurants. Avoid any inconvenience by locating nearby public restrooms beforehand or visiting a cafe or restaurant that offers restroom access for patrons.

Check Outdoor Seating Fees near Plaza Mayor

If you choose to sit at one of the outdoor cafes or restaurants in Plaza Mayor, be aware that there may be additional fees for table service or "coperto." Avoid any surprises by confirming these fees before sitting down and ordering.

Don't Forget to Watch the Sunset Over the City

Regardless of whether you will be in Salamanca for a couple of days or only 24 hours, don't forget to take in the sunset over the city. It's a beautiful sight to watch the buildings start to illuminate as the sun sets for the day, and it is Instagram photo-worthy!

Don't Forget to Check the Dress Code

Some religious sites in Salamanca, such as cathedrals and churches, have dress codes requiring visitors to dress modestly. Avoid being turned away by dressing appropriately, which typically means covering shoulders and knees.

Don't Forget to Visit Hidden Courtyard and Plaza in Old Town

The Old Town of Salamanca is dotted with charming courtyards, hidden plazas, and secluded gardens, providing tranquil spots to relax and admire the architecture. Avoid missing these hidden gems by exploring beyond the main streets and squares.

Next Stop: Cádiz

Although Salamanca is smaller than some of Spain's other cities, it's arguably one of the most beautiful ones to see while visiting the country. You'll immediately immerse yourself in the rich architecture of the Plaza Mayor and the cathedrals, giving you a glimpse into the city's old life.

In the next chapter, we will spend some time in Cádiz, a beautiful town on the Iberian Peninsula. This city has seen its fair share of history, including the Napoleonic wars.

Chapter 7:

Cadiz—Dos and Don'ts

C ádiz is one of Europe's oldest cities, dating back to 1100 B.C.E.; the Phoenicians founded it as "Gadir." Since then, it has seen its fair share of history, from the many nations inhabiting its land (Carthaginians, Visigoths, Romans, and Muslims) to the daring and constant pirate attacks and invasions. Cádiz even saw the famous Italian Explorer Christopher Columbus set sail on the Atlantic Ocean in 1493 to explore the world!

Discovering Cadiz

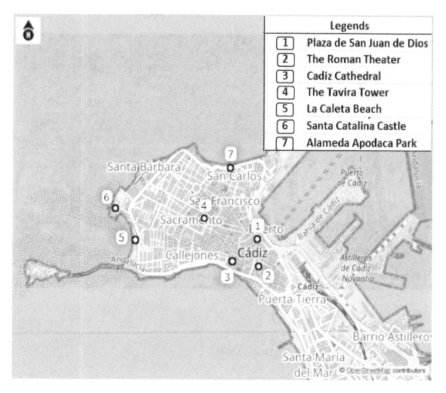

Legends	
1	Plaza de San Juan de Dios
2	The Roman Theater
3	Cadiz Cathedral
4	The Tavira Tower
5	La Caleta Beach
6	Santa Catalina Castle
7	Alameda Apodaca Park

Cádiz may be old, but it is arguably another of Spain's underrated cities to explore. Situated along the ocean, it is one of Spain's leading port cities (one of the most important ones) and has plenty of well-preserved landmarks to see. There are plenty of beautiful beaches to explore, picturesque plazas surrounded by stunning architecture, and so many narrow winding streets to get lost in. Visiting this little slice of land will give you an idea of what life has had through the centuries. There is a lot more to see and do than meets the eye!

What to Do in Cádiz

The Plaza de San Juan de Dios

The Plaza de San Juan de Dios is in the heart of Cádiz and is the most significant in the city. In its earlier days, it was the place for markets and trading goods from the Americas. By the 18th century, several buildings were constructed and reflected the Elizabethan and Baroque styles. Cádiz's Town Hall, the Church of San Juan Dios, and the Casa de los Pazos Miranda are in this square. This is a great starting point for your other adventures in this coastal city (and perfect for photo opportunities).

The Roman Theater

Address: Calle Mesón, 11, 13, 11005 Cádiz
Hours of operation
- Monday to Friday: 11 a.m. to 5 p.m.
  - o   Closes at 4:30 p.m. between September and April.
- Saturday and Sunday: 10 a.m. to 2 p.m.

The Roman Theater (Teatro Romano) is an ancient site in Cádiz that wasn't uncovered until the 1980s. Archaeologists believe the theater was built sometime in the first or second century, and its impressive size is the largest Roman theater ever built. Its diameter is 120 meters, and at the time, it would have held between 10,000 and 20,000 people to watch the events. Further examination of the theater also revealed that it was used until at least the 17th century.

This is a free attraction to check out. You'll be able to explore some of the excavated theater. You should also visit the interpretation center, which will give you more history of the theater and the ongoing excavations.

Cadiz Cathedral

Address: Plaza de la Catedral, 11005 Cádiz

Hours of operation: The cathedral is open from 10 a.m. to 7 p.m. Monday to Saturday and from 1:30 p.m. to 7 p.m. on Sunday. The last admission is at 6:15 p.m. If you intend to visit the Clock Tower, the hours are Monday to Saturday. On Sundays, you can climb the clock tower between 12 p.m. and 3 p.m. and from 3:30 p.m. to 7 p.m. The last admission to the clock tower is 30 minutes before closing.

Cádiz Cathedral is one of the most iconic buildings in Cádiz. Construction on this stunning cathedral began in the 18th century and took 116 years. As such, the interior has a mix of Baroque, Rococo, and Neoclassical styles, showcasing the cathedral's changing design throughout the centuries.

There are many things to see in this cathedral. Its stunning high ceilings, the golden dome that reflects the gorgeous Spanish sun, and the tombs of two influential figures in Cádiz's history, composer Manuel de Falla and writer José María Permán. However, the Clock Tower is one of the most impressive areas in this cathedral. This tower opened to the public in 2015 and gives you some of the most breathtaking views of the Atlantic Ocean, the harbor, and Cádiz's city center.

Ticket type	Price
General Admission	€ 7
Seniors	€ 6
Students (13 to 25 years old)	€ 5
Children 12 and under	Free

The Tavira Tower

Address: C. Marqués del Real Tesoro, 10, 11001 Cádiz

Hours of operation

- October to April: 10 a.m. to 6 p.m. (the last admission time is at 6 p.m.)
- May to September: 10 a.m. to 8 p.m. (the last admission time is at 7 p.m.)

The watchtowers in Cádiz once served as the place for people to watch prosperity and trade in the port during the 18th century—the Tavira Tower (Torre Tavira) was the official tower for this purpose since it is in the heart of the city and is the highest watchtower of the many throughout Cádiz. As the goods came in from America, the watchmen would keep an eye on everything going on using a telescope.

Climbing the tower will allow you to put yourself into the shoes of the watchmen, taking in the beautiful scenery of Cádiz's harbor and other city views. Additionally, you can see some scenes projected onto a screen from a Camera Obscura to see the development throughout the centuries to where the port is today.

Ticket type	Price
Adults	€ 8
Students (with valid ID), seniors 65 years old and up, and large families	€ 6

La Caleta Beach

La Caleta Beach is a beautiful cove between Santa Catalina and San Sebastián Castles. It is a popular place to cool off in the summer and to watch the sunset, which creates perfect picture opportunities.

Santa Catalina Castle

Address: C. Campo de las Balas, s/n, 11002 Cádiz

Hours of operation

- Summer hours (mid-June to mid-September)
  - Monday to Saturday: 10 a.m. to 2 p.m. and 5 p.m. to 9 p.m.
  - Sunday: 10 a.m. to 3 p.m.
  - Feast days and Sunday eve's ahead of holiday Mondays: 10 a.m. to 2 p.m. and 5 p.m. to 9 p.m.
- Winter hours (mid-September to mid-June)
  - Monday to Saturday: 10 a.m. to 6 p.m.
  - Sunday: 10 a.m. to 3 p.m.
  - Feast days and Sunday eve's ahead of holiday Mondays: 10 a.m. to 6 p.m.
- All hours are subject to change based on the time of the year, so your best bet for planning is to verify the hours on their website.

Santa Catalina Castle (Castillo de Santa Catalina) is Cádiz's oldest military fortress, dating back to the 1590s; however, its origins date even further back to when the

Muslims first occupied the Iberian Peninsula, with walls built on a hill between the eighth and ninth centuries—some of this original fortress can still be seen today.

When the Christians took over Cádiz (then Jaén) in the 13th century, they reinforced the Islamic walls and created a new fortress. They further expanded the castle, renaming it Santa Catalina Castle by the 15th century. During the two-year War of Independence, the Napoleonic army took over the castle as their headquarters. During that period, the castle underwent some changes. However, when the troops left, they damaged some fortresses by blowing up large parts of them.

The government worked to restore this important monument in the 20th century. Today, you can walk around the castle and take in its former life. It's also worth exploring their interpretive center, which will give you more about the history of Santa Catalina Castle.

Ticket type	Price
Adults	€ 3.50
Seniors (65 years old and up), children (4 to 12 years old), students, disabled visitors, and large families	€ 1.50
Adult night activities	€ 8

Admission is free on Wednesdays between 5 p.m. and 9 p.m. during the summer hours and from 3 p.m. to 6 p.m.

Alameda Apodaca Park

Alameda Apodaca Park is a beautiful public space near Cádiz's city center. It faces the South Bay and other nearby towns.

The park is famous for its stunning gardens, fountains, and statues, covering 45,000 square meters. As you explore and enjoy this beautiful space, you'll be rewarded with gorgeous views of the Atlantic Ocean and the surrounding area.

This park also features several busts for history buffs to honor Latin America's influential figures. You can find them along the Balcony of the Bay of Cádiz, including

- Nicaraguan poet Rubén Darío
- the Grand Admiral of Peru, Don Miguel Grau Seminario
- Cuban politician and poet José Marti
- Dominical politician and liberalor: Juan Pablo Duarte
- Chilean General José Miguel Carrera
- Deputy of the Cortes of Cadiz and Puerto Rican sailor Ramón Power y Giralt

What Festivals to Enjoy in Cádiz

Easter Week

If you're in Cádiz during the week of Easter, you're in for a treat. Cádiz goes all out to celebrate this holiday. The city is decked out for the event, with many celebrations and processions. This event attracts thousands to this coastal town annually to watch the floats and religious sculptures through the winding, narrow streets. There is also plenty of live music, most notably "The Seven Last Words of Christ" composed by Joseph Haydn.

The Cádiz Carnival

Carnival in Spain is a fun festival to attend. However, in Cádiz, the scene is lively with bright colors, live music, dancing, and parades marching through the winding streets. As you may recall, Carnival is a time for people to get together before Lent. If you're in Cádiz during this time, immerse yourself in this cultural event because the energy will be unlike anything you have ever experienced.

Where to Eat in Cádiz

Cádiz has plenty of tapas restaurants to explore and try. Given that this city is on a small piece of land surrounded by the ocean, you can expect that Cádiz restaurants will have an array of seafood options!

Restaurante Mirador Las Cortes

Address: Calle San Francisco, 9, 11004 Cádiz
Restaurante Mirador Las Cortes is a budget-friendly option for traditional Spanish food in Cádiz. It also accommodates gluten-free diners.

Bar el Veedor

Address: Calle veedor Esq, C. Vea Murguía, 10, 11003 Cádiz
Bar el Veedor is an excellent tapas spot to eat. Their menu has many options, including seafood, cold cuts, and other Spanish specialties to satisfy your cravings. If you love to drink sherry, they pour this from a wooden barrel, giving you a distinct flavor. Prices here are great as well!

El Tío de la Tiza

Address: Plaza del Tío de la Tiza 12, 11002 Cadiz
El Tío de la Tiza offers some of the best seafood in the city. It's also one of the most popular spots, so reservations are necessary. The dishes are made with fresh ingredients, and the restaurant can accommodate gluten-free and vegetarian diets.

Candela

Address: 11001, C. Feduchy, 3, 11001 Cádiz
For a fancier night out, check out Candela. This tapas restaurant offers generous portions for your food choices. Many people love this restaurant for their presentation. One of the most popular options on the menu is their octopus with potatoes and seaweed cream.

Recreo Chico

Address: Calle Ancha 9, 11001 Cadiz Spain
Recreo Chico will make you feel like an honored guest. This restaurant is owned by two women who take the time to walk you through their menu, personalizing the experience. They offer traditional Spanish meals as well as some international ones.

What to Eat in Cádiz

Pescaíto Frito

Cádiz is renowned for its pescaíto frito, a variety of small fish that are seasoned, coated in flour, and deep-fried until crispy. Popular choices include boquerones (anchovies), chipirones (baby squid), and adobo (marinated fish). Enjoy these delightful bites as a tapa or part of a larger meal.

Salmorejo

While salmorejo is a dish more commonly associated with Andalusia in general, it's worth trying in Cádiz. This cold soup is made from tomatoes, bread, olive oil, garlic, and vinegar, creating a thick and refreshing concoction. It's often garnished with hard-boiled eggs and jamón (cured ham).

Chocos a la Gaditana

Cuttlefish is a popular seafood choice in Cádiz, and chocos a la Gaditana is a local preparation that showcases this ingredient. The cuttlefish is typically stewed with onions, garlic, tomatoes, and a variety of spices, resulting in a flavorful and tender dish.

Tortillitas de Camarones

Tortillitas de camarones are small shrimp fritters, a specialty in Cádiz. The batter is made with chickpea flour, water, and tiny shrimp, creating a crispy and savory treat. These fritters are often enjoyed as a tapa or appetizer.

Cazón en Adobo (Marinated Dogfish)

Cazón en adobo is a popular dish featuring marinated dogfish, a type of shark. The fish is marinated in a flavorful mixture of garlic, oregano, cumin, vinegar, and paprika before being deep-fried. It's commonly served as a tapa or in a sandwich, known as bocadillo de cazón.

Where to Stay in Cádiz

The wonderful thing about Cádiz is how small it is—you can easily walk to all the landmarks from any accommodation you choose! Here are some of the places to consider staying at while in Cádiz.

Hotel Regio

Address: Avenida Ana de Viya, 11 11009 Cádiz

If you're planning a trip to Cádiz to have a beach day or two, the Hotel Regio is a great accommodation option. This hotel is by the Playa de la Victoria, Cádiz's most extensive beach, where you can enjoy the warm Spanish sun or water sports in the crystal blue water. Additionally, Hotel Regio has plenty of bars and restaurants nearby and is about 20 minutes from the town center. Prices are about mid-range for this hotel, and some rooms have a balcony and a fridge.

Senator Cádiz Spa Hotel

Address: Rubio y Díaz, 1, 11004 Cádiz

Who doesn't want a little pampering while on vacation? You might be going to Cádiz to explore its beautiful city, but it doesn't hurt to treat yourself occasionally.

Senator Cádiz Spa Hotel is in a restored stately home across from the port. The spa is below the hotel and has Turkish and Indo-Roman baths, spray rain, saunas, and, for the brave, a cold-water foot bath and an ice cave. The spa is open Tuesday through Sunday from 10 a.m. to 2 p.m. and 5 p.m. to 9 p.m.

The hotel is about a 10-minute walk from the heart of Cádiz. All rooms have modern furniture, beautiful windows, and wooden floors. This accommodation offers a luxurious stay, so prices are higher.

Hotel Convento Cádiz

Address: Calle Santo Domingo 2, 11006 Cadiz

Hotel Convento Cádiz is a stunning boutique hotel in a beautiful 17th-century former convent. The rooms are spacious and comfortable. However, one of the prime spots of Hotel Convento Cádiz is its courtyard with its beautiful arches and marble pillars.

Location-wise, this hotel is near several of Cádiz's historical landmarks, so you won't need to walk too far to take public transportation!

Boutique Hotel OLOM

Address: Plaza de la Catedral, 9, 11005 Cádiz

Boutique Hotel OLOM is another luxury option in Cádiz. This stunning hotel is adjacent to the Santa Cruz Cathedral, which overlooks the rooftop terrace. Speaking of which, this rooftop terrace has an infinity jacuzzi pool and a rooftop bar to enjoy. Please note that this hotel is not recommended for traveling with children.

Hotel Monte Puertatierra

Address: Avenida Andalucía, 34, 11008 Cádiz Spain

Hotel Monte Puertatierra is another great accommodation option if you plan to spend your time at the beach. This hotel is near Playa Santa Maria and Playa de la Victoria, where you can enjoy various beach activities. If you want to take a break from the beach, this hotel is about 10 minutes from historical landmarks, including the Tavira Tower, the Roman Theater, and the cathedral.

As for the rooms, they are all spacious and allow plenty of natural light. They are fitted with modern amenities as well.

Hotel Argantonio

Address: Calle Argantonio 3, 11004 Cadiz

Hotel Aragantonio is in the lovely San Carlos neighborhood and steps from many of Cádiz's landmarks, including the Alameda Apodaca Park (Almada de Apodaca) and the Plaza España. This hotel has plenty of room options for families or if you're traveling solo or with a partner. If you're traveling with family, it's worth it to book one of their apartments, which has a fully equipped kitchen and a private terrace to enjoy.

La Posada del Mercado

Address: C. José de Dios, 9, 11001 Cádiz

La Posada del Mercado is an excellent option if you want to stay in a self-accommodating option. These apartments are budget-friendly and come in different sizes. They even have washing machines if you need to do laundry or plan to be in Cádiz for a week or two.

The closest beach to this accommodation is La Caleta Beach. Many landmarks and other attractions in the city are also within walking distance.

Hotel Las Cortes de Cádiz

Address: Calle San Francisco, 9, 11004 Cadiz

Hotel Las Cortes de Cádiz is in a renovated 19th-century building. It is a three-minute walk from the port and 10 minutes from the city center by transportation.

This hotel is mid-range, offers a continental breakfast, and has a rooftop terrace with great views of Cádiz.

The hotel's interior is beautiful and well-reflects its former life. All rooms are very bright and welcoming for any type of traveler. Some rooms have a balcony, while others overlook the inner courtyard. This hotel also offers family-sized rooms.

Parador de Cádiz

Address: Avenida Duque de Nájera, 9, 11002 Cádiz

Parador de Cádiz is a luxury option, with a spa and pools overlooking Cádiz's oceanfront. Most rooms have floor-to-ceiling windows that look onto the Atlantic Ocean and balconies to enjoy morning coffee. La Caleta Beach is the closest beach to this hotel, and the train station is just under two miles away.

Hotel Patagonia Sur

Address: Cobos, 11, 11005 Cádiz

Check out Hotel Patagonia Sur for more stylish and contemporary accommodation. This hotel is within walking distance of many historical landmarks, including the cathedral. It is also close to the harbor, where you can catch a ferry to the Canary Islands, El Puerto, and Rota. The rooms are tastefully decorated with beautiful oak floors and abstract artwork and equipped with a minibar.

What Not to Do in Cádiz

Don't Feel the Need to Drive in Cádiz

Cádiz is small enough to walk to various points of interest easily. You'll save yourself the headache of navigating the narrow streets and finding parking while allowing yourself to take in everything this beautiful port city has to offer. Additionally, there is a high-speed rail network you can use, too!

Don't Underestimate the Wind

There will be some days when the wind is stronger than anticipated. Remember to check weather reports for wind warnings, especially if you intend to visit one of Cáziz's beaches!

Don't Expect Cold Weather in the Winter

One of the beautiful things about Cádiz is that it is in Southern Spain and typically has warm temperatures year-round! So, to enjoy some winter sun, consider spending a week in this Spanish town, as temperatures can reach as high as 62 °F.

Don't Miss Sunset at La Caleta

La Caleta is one of Cadiz's most iconic beaches, offering breathtaking sunset views over the Atlantic Ocean. Avoid missing this magical moment by taking a leisurely stroll along the beachfront promenade or enjoying a drink at one of the nearby cafes.

Don't Miss Exploring Beyond the Square at Plaza de San Juan de Dios

While Plaza de San Juan de Dios is undoubtedly charming, don't limit yourself to just the square. Explore the surrounding streets and alleys, which are full of hidden gems, local shops, and cafes.

Dress Appropriately While Visiting Cadiz Cathedral

The Cadiz Cathedral is a religious site, and visitors are expected to dress modestly. Avoid being turned away by wearing appropriate attire, such as clothing that covers shoulders and knees, and refraining from wearing beachwear or revealing clothing.

Next Stop: Granada

Cádiz's ancient and fascinating history offers more time to explore the country's origins. From the Roman Theater to the Santa Catalina Castle, there is much to learn about how Cádiz is a significant city in Spain.

In the next chapter, we will explore Granada, Spain's largest urban city, which has seen thousands of tourists even in the last few years!

Chapter 8:

Granada—Dos and Don'ts

O f all the cities in Spain, Granada is the fifth most visited one—not just for its rich history but also because it is one of the best places to ski! Before COVID-19, over 5 million people explored its streets and mountains; despite restrictions, 2.6 million people visited in 2021! Why is this city a popular option compared to others we have explored? Let's find out.

Discovering Granada

Granada's history extends back to the seventh century when the Iberians first inhabited the city. However, what makes this city famous is more than Europe's southernmost place to ski most of the year, where the Sierra Nevada's peaks are snow-capped between November and May. You can also expect plenty of sun in Granada as it's sunny nearly every day, but also for its Moorish architecture.

This city has also played an essential role in Islamic culture as it has been the home of Muslims longer than any other place in Europe. In fact, the Moors helped Granada become known to other explorers of the world, becoming Nasrid Kingdom's capital. When the Catholic Monarchs came into the city in 1492, Muslims and the Jewish people who lived there were either forced to convert their faith or leave. Three UNESCO World Heritage Sites are great examples of Granada, two of which we'll explore more in-depth.

As for the local dialect, Granada is in one of the eight Andalusian provinces in Spain. Spanish will be understood, but their language variation is Andalusian Spanish.

There is so much to do, eat, and enjoy in this city, so let's discover what you should do in Granada.

What to Do in Granada

Alhambra

Address: C. Real de la Alhambra, s/n, Centro, 18009 Granada

Hours of operation

- April 1 to October 14: 1) Day visits: 8:30 a.m. to 8 p.m. daily, 2) Evening visits: 8 p.m. to 11:30 p.m. daily (the ticket office closes at 10:45 p.m.)
- October 15 to March 31: 1) Day visits: 8:30 a.m. to 6 p.m. daily, 2) Evening visits: 8 p.m. to 11:30 p.m. daily (the ticket office closes at 10:45 p.m.)

The magnificent palace of Alhambra is a site to behold. This fortress was once a royal home that dates back to the mid-13th century (though its initial design was to be used for military purposes). The intricate carvings and colorful tiles are a great example of Islamic architecture from that era. This is a must-visit because of how different Alhambra is from some of the more traditional architecture you would see elsewhere in Spain. This visit will also give you insight into what Spain was like before it became the country we know today.

You can purchase entrance tickets to explore the palace on your own. However, their website does not provide that information, so you must buy them at their ticket office. However, it's highly recommended to take a guided tour (tickets start at €39 per person) as you'll be able to explore the various rooms of the palace as well as the Generalife Gardens and the Nasrid Palaces.

Generalife Gardens

The Generalife Gardens are part of Alhambra, which visitors can explore while visiting the ancient fortress. These gardens date back to the 13th century and served as a tranquil retreat for the Nasrid rulers of Granada. In this garden, you will see numerous courtyards to explore, all adorned with stunning fountains or other water features, terraces, and lush greenery. Additionally, some stunning archways reflect Islamic architecture, offering visitors a glimpse into the golden ages of Granada.

The tickets to the gardens are included with your admission to Alhambra.

Capilla Real de Granada

Address: Calle Oficios, s/n, 18001 Granada, Spain

Hours of operation

- Monday to Saturday: 10 a.m. to 6:30 p.m.
- Sunday: 11 a.m. to 6:30 p.m.

Like Alhambra, the Capilla Real de Granada (Royal Chapel of Granada) is another place in Granada that is a testament to the city's rich history and heritage. Catholic monarchs Queen Isabella I and King Ferdinand II saw Granada as their final resting place and, as such, had this chapel constructed for them. This stunning chapel was completed in the 16th century and reflects Gothic and Renaissance architecture throughout its walls. More interesting is the juxtaposition between the Christian and Moorish religions, given its proximity to the Alhambra.

As you explore the chapel, you will see the intricate details of the building and a collection of religious art, Italian and Spanish Paintings, the queen's books, tapestries, and gold and silver work in their Sacristy museum.

Ticket type	Price
Adults	€ 6
Students (13 to 25 years old)	€ 4.50
Children 12 and under	Free

Some rules to keep in mind when you are visiting the Capilla Real de Granada:

- You must remain quiet when you are visiting the temple.
- Turn your phone on silent.
- Don't wear hats in the temple.
- Don't take photos inside the temple.

Catedral Santa María de la Encarnación

Address: C. Gran Vía de Colón, 5, Centro, 18001 Granada, Spain

Hours of operation

- Monday to Saturday from 10 a.m. to 6:15 p.m.
- Sunday: 3 p.m. to 6:15 p.m.

Catedral Santa María de la Encarnación is another excellent example of religious architecture in Granada. It was constructed between the 16th and 18th centuries and blended Gothic, Renaissance, and Baroque styles inside and out.

When you enter the chapel, you'll be amazed by the tall columns extending up to the ceiling, intricate carvings, and stunning golden altarpieces. You will also admire several of the chapel's artworks by renowned Spanish artist Alonso Cano. While here, you should also explore the tombs as this is where you will see the tombs of Queen Isabella I and King Ferdinand II.

Ticket type	Price
Adults	€ 6
Students (13 to 25 years old)	€ 4.50
Children 12 and under	Free

Since the royal chapel is within the same complex, you can buy a combined ticket that will give you access to both monuments.

El Bañuelo

Address: Carrera del Darro, 31, Albaicín, 18010 Granada

Hours of operation: 10 a.m. to 5 p.m. daily

El Bañuelo is one of Granada's hidden gems that will bring you back in time to the city's Moorish heritage. This amazingly preserved Arab bathhouse dates back to the 11th century, showcasing some of Granda's most authentic examples of Islamic architecture. When you visit El Bañuelo, you'll be transported back in time as you wander through the stunning chambers fitted with arched doorways, stucco decorations, and star-shaped skylights that allow the sunlight to illuminate the space.

This attraction is free to visit and can be accessed through the former Christian home.

La Cartuja Monastery

Address: P.º de Cartuja, s/n, Beiro, 18011 Granada

Hours of operation

- Sunday to Friday: 10 a.m. to 7 p.m.
- Saturday: 10 a.m. to 12:45 p.m. and 3 p.m. to 6 p.m.

La Cartuja Monastery is another great hidden gem in Granada. It dates back to the 16th century and is a testament to some of Spain's finest Baroque architecture. As it took a few centuries to complete, there are also notes of Gothic and Renaissance within its walls.

The monastery has many significant areas to explore, but the church, cloisters, and courtyards are some of the top highlights. Inside the church, you will want to explore the Sacristy, where the monks would prepare for mass. It is sacred and stunning, with the Baroque details on the wall and ceiling paintings.

This is a great place to visit if you're seeking a tranquil setting to explore and learn more about Granada's rich religious history.

Corral de Carbòn

Address: Calle Mariana Pineda, Edificio Corral del Carbón, s/n, 18009, Granada

Hours of operation: 9 a.m. to 8 p.m. daily

The Corral de Carbòn is the oldest Arab monument in Granada, dating back to the 14th century. This monument gives us another glimpse into Granada's Moorish history. At one point, it served as an accommodation for traveling merchants and their goods. In the 16th century, it became a place for theater performances.

This monument is a bookshop today, but you can enjoy courtyard performances in the summer or explore the inner courtyard and admire the architecture.

What Festivals to Enjoy in Granada

Festival of Granada

The Festival of Granada happens yearly between June and July at various venues across Granada. You can enjoy many performances at this festival, including a symphony at the Palace of Charles V, ballet performances in the Generalife Gardens open-air theater, and the Patio de Los Arrayanes at Alhambra.

Tickets and the different performance dates and times can be found on the festival's website if you want to immerse yourself in Granada's artistic heritage.

Fiesta de la Toma

Every January 2, the Fiesta de la Toma commemorates Granada's capture by Catholic Monarchs Ferdinand II of Aragon and Isabella I of Castille. During this festival, you can participate in many activities, including parades, traditional music and dance, religious ceremonies, and reenactments of the historical day. It is a great way to learn more about Granada's rich history and celebrate its cultural heritage.

Fiesta de San Cecilio

The Fiesta de San Cecilio happens annually on the first weekend of February in Granada to celebrate the city's patron saint, Saint San Cecilio. San Cecilio is believed to have been one of the three disciples sent for evangelization by St. Peter. Cecilio, along with nine other priests, gathered in the catacombs near a mountain; they were surrounded by the Romans and killed.

You will see religious processions, traditional music performances, and other cultural events during this festival. This is a great way to participate in Granada's traditions and pay homage to its patron saint.

Cruces de Mayo

Cruces de Mayo (May of Crosses) festival is a vibrant celebration in Granada's first week of May. This festival dates back to 1625 to celebrate a cross installed in the San Lázaro district. If you attend this festival, you can expect to see plenty of religious and folk traditions, beautifully decorated crosses, and altars adorned with floral arrangements, pottery, and copper objects.

Fería de Granada

Fería de Granada (Fair of Granada) is one of Granada's most eagerly awaited events to take place in this city. This festival happens around the end of May or the start of June and is a week long. During this festival, there are plenty of activities to immerse yourself in, including parades, flamenco dancing, bullfights, and live music. This is one of Granada's most lively festivals, so be sure to check the dates to see if they align with your trip dates because you won't want to miss them!

Where to Eat in Granada

Granada's food scene is a fusion of Spanish and North African flavors, with dishes like paella, kebabs, and gazpacho. However, even if you aren't eating out, it's customary and is just stopping in for a quick drink; it's customary to have free tapas served with your beverage!

Restaurante Más Que Vinos

Address: Calle Tundidores 10 With Calle Zacatin – Bajo, 18001 Granada

Restaurante Más Que Vinos is a hidden gem hidden from Granada's main streets. This place has a great selection of wine for great prices to pair with your tapas. They can also accommodate those with vegetarian, vegan, and gluten-free dietary needs.

Pastelería López-Mezquita

Address: Calle de los Reyes Católicos 39, 18001 Granada

One of Granada's specialties is a pionono: A delicious rolled pastry with jelly in the middle. If you want to try this delightful delicacy alongside a coffee or tea, go to the Pastelería López-Mezquita to pick up this sweet treat. This restaurant also serves breakfast or brunch as well.

Taberna La Tana

Address: Calle Virgen del Rosario 11 Bajo, Esquina Placeta del Agua, 18009 Granada

Taberna La Tana is another hidden gem in Granada for great restaurants, serving plenty of wine by the glass and a massive food selection. It's best to book a table ahead of time if you plan to go because it can get quite busy!

Bar Los Diamantes

Address: Calle Navas 28, 18009 Granada

Bar Los Diamantes is famous for its tapas, particularly fried fish. This restaurant is a little more expensive if you want a nice meal. However, if you are trying to save money, consider stopping here for a quick drink with a side of tapas.

Om Kalsum

Address: Calle Jardines 17, 18002 Granada

For a different flavor fusion, Om Kalsum serves up Moroccan-flavored tapas. This is a popular place, with many waiting to get in. People love the great menu options and the fantastic customer service!

What to Eat in Granada

Tapa of Free Tapas

In Granada, it's a tradition for many bars to serve a free tapa (small appetizer) with each drink you order. The city is famous for its generous tapas culture, where you can enjoy a variety of complimentary snacks ranging from olives and almonds to more elaborate dishes like patatas bravas (fried potatoes with spicy tomato sauce).

Huevos Rotos

Huevos rotos is a popular dish consisting of fried potatoes topped with a layer of fried eggs. The dish gets its name from the tradition of breaking the yolks over the potatoes, creating a rich and satisfying combination. It's often served with ham or chorizo.

Pipirrana

Pipirrana is a refreshing Andalusian salad that typically includes tomatoes, green peppers, onions, and cucumbers, all finely chopped and dressed with olive oil and vinegar. It's a perfect dish to enjoy during the warm weather, offering a burst of flavors.

Remojón Granadino

Remojón Granadino is a traditional salad featuring salted cod, oranges, olives, and hard-boiled eggs. The combination of sweet and savory flavors makes it a unique and delightful dish, especially during the spring and summer months.

Where to Stay in Granada

Hotel Casa 1800 Granada

Address: Benalua, 11 (Plaza Nueva), Albaicín, 18010 Granada

If you're looking for a place that will put you close to many of the landmarks in Granada, book a room with Hotel Casa 1800. This boutique hotel has comfortable double rooms (some with a private terrace). If you are traveling with a family and need an additional bed, it will be added to your room fee.

NH Collection Victoria

Address: Puerta Real, 3, Granada City Centre, 18005 Granada

Set in a 19th-century building, the NH Collection Victoria is right in the heart of Granada, putting you within steps of the city's landmarks. Each room has the essentials, including a coffee or tea maker and a minibar. Several room options are available, and you can expect the room prices to be mid-to-higher.

Porcel Navas

Address: Navas, 22, Granada City Centre, 18009 Granada

If you want to surround yourself with a lively restaurant atmosphere to enjoy nights out, Porcel Navas is a great option. This hotel offers several room options, including family-sized rooms. It's also central to many of Granada's landmarks.

Parador de Granada

Address: Real de la Alhambra, s/n, Granada City Centre, 18009 Granada

If you want to be closer to the Alhambra palace, Parador de Granada is the only place within this area for accommodation purposes. Staying here will also take you back to the 15th century, as the hotel was once a convent! This accommodation is the most expensive option, but the rooms are beautiful and have many amenities. You'll also have great views of landmarks and the surrounding area, and you can sit on their gorgeous terrace that overlooks the Alhambra's gardens.

Gar Anat Hotel Boutique

Address: Placeta de los Peregrinos, 1, Granada City Centre, 18009 Granada

Gar Anat Hotel Boutique is set in the Realejo neighborhood (famous for its street art). This hotel is in a 17th-century building with a stunning interior displaying some of its former life with modern touches. The rooms are spacious and bright, and the staff is helpful and can book reservations for you if needed!

Palacio De Los Navas

Address: Navas, 1, Granada City Centre, 18009 Granada

For a more budget-friendly option in the Realejo neighborhood, the Palacio De Los Nevas will put you within walking distance of Granada's landmarks without breaking your budget. This hotel is in a 16th-century building with bright rooms overlooking the courtyard. This is an excellent option for solo travelers, as they have rooms with a single bed.

Hotel Boutique Puerta de las Granadas

Address: Cuesta de Gomérez 16, Granada City Centre, 18009 Granada

Hotel Boutique Puerta de las Granadas is in a former 19th-century building at the foot of the Alhambra, a short walk from the Granada Cathedral. The hotel has an excellent on-site restaurant that can accommodate dietary needs, and family rooms are available.

Candil Suite Realego

Address: Cuesta Del Realejo ,22, Granada City Centre, 18009 Granada

Candil Suite Realego is a bed and breakfast option offering beautiful views of the mountains in the distance. This accommodation is near the Generalife and Alhambra landmarks. They also have bicycles you can hire for a day of exploring the city if you do not want to walk everywhere!

Florentia Homes

Address: 7 Calle San Nicolas, Albaicin, 18010 Granada

Florentia Homes is a self-catering option if you prefer this over a hotel. These apartments are a short walk from the San Nicholas viewpoint. All apartments are equipped with a kitchenette, and some include views of the mountains and a balcony or patio.

Pension Venecia Gomerez

Address: Cuesta Gomérez, 2, Granada City Centre, 18009 Granada

Situated in the guest house, the Pension Venecia Gomerez is one of the most budget-friendly accommodations to look into while in Granada. This is a guest house, so not every room has a private bathroom. However, all rooms have a private balcony to enjoy. They also have family room options.

What Not to Do in Granada

Don't Buy Cheap Taracea Souvenirs

You'll see souvenirs wherever you travel—that is a given! In Granada, you may see wooden boxes used to decorate furniture. The ancient crafting of this is called taracea and involves using a mosaic of wooden pieces. However, most souvenir places will sell cheap replicas of them. So, if you're looking for a taracea box, you can find them along Cuesta de Gomerez and Cuesta Marañas. Pro tip: Check for an authenticity stamp on the bottom to ensure it's the real deal!

Don't Drive in Granada

We spoke about this tip in the last chapter. Granada also has plenty of narrow streets, which are tricky to navigate if you're unfamiliar with them. Most places are within walking distance if not a short bus ride away! So, if you have rented a car, consider leaving it at your accommodation.

Don't Wait to Get Your Tickets to Alhambra

Alhambra is a popular attraction in Granada and the best to experience on a guided tour. To avoid disappointment, book tickets at least 10 days in advance.

Next Stop: Valencia

While Granada may not have been on your list of places to see in Spain, this chapter has now introduced you to this vibrant and different city. It's in this city where you will get to immerse yourself in a different kind of history that helped shape Spain into the country it is today.

In the next chapter, we are going to explore Valencia, another ancient Spanish city rich with history dating back to the Roman era and many evolutions throughout its years.

Chapter 9:

Valencia—Dos and Don'ts

T he enchanting city of València is one of the oldest cities in Spain, with roots dating back to the Roman period in the year 138. Over time, this city has seen many changes through the conquests of the Visigoths and Moors. Still, the city's depth was not known until 1985, when excavations revealed more about the city's origins. The findings from the excavations subsequently opened up a distinctive museum behind the cathedral. As you explore this city, you will see its life as it is now and as it once was by wandering along the two main roads that once connected it.

Discovering València

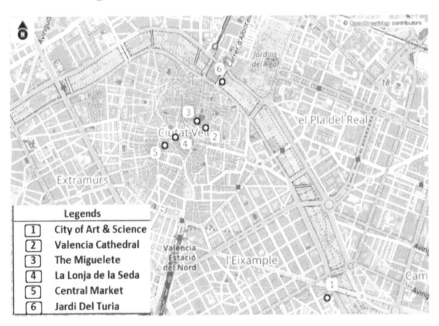

Legends

1	City of Art & Science
2	Valencia Cathedral
3	The Miguelete
4	La Lonja de la Seda
5	Central Market
6	Jardi Del Turia

València's history and culture are rich, and what is so remarkable about this city is how it weaves everything that makes València what it is. As you explore its ancient roots, you'll follow the footsteps of the Romans, Visigoths, and Moors, each leaving their mark on this city. While the history of this city is amazing to experience and explore, València also has a stunning landscape; from its beautiful sunny beaches to the gorgeous gardens and the Turia River, you'll find a picturesque backdrop wherever you end up.

As València has been shaped by centuries of civilizations, its culture is brimming with a unique heritage where you can immerse yourself. In València, you'll find a lively display of afternoon fireworks in early March and the vibrant Las Fallas festival that will set this city apart from other cities in Spain. Let's explore what is so captivating about València and how this can make your travel experience unforgettable.

What to Do in València

City of the Arts and Sciences

Address: Av. Del Professor López Piñero 7, 46013 València

Hours of operation: The City of the Arts and Sciences hours vary throughout the year and weeks. It is best to check the website to determine the best days for you as you book your tickets.

The City of Arts and Sciences is an impressive piece of 21st-century architecture that displays innovation and modernity. This futuristic complex has plenty of things to do and experience within its six buildings, blending art, science, and technology. In the Hemisfèric, you can watch IMAX and digital films, the Umbacle gives you a significant landscaped vantage point, explore science in the Príncipe

Felipe Science Museum, see over 500 marine species in the Oceanogràfic, and take in opera or concerts at the Reina Sofía Palace of the Arts and the Ágora.

Science Museum (Museu de les Ciències)

Ticket type	Price
General admission (13 years old and up)	€ 9
Children (4 to 12 years old) and seniors (65 years old and up)	€ 6.90
Children under 3	Free

Hemispheric (Hemisfèric)

Ticket type	Price
General admission (13 years old and up)	€ 8.70
Children (4 to 12 years old) and seniors (65 years old and up)	€ 6.70
Children under 3	Free

Oceanogràfic (Oceanografic)

Ticket type	Price
General admission (13 years old and up)	€ 34.70
Children (4 to 12 years old) and seniors (65 years old and up)	€ 25.75
Children under 3	Free

Casco Histórico

Casco Histórico is the historic old town of València that will transport you back in time. As you wander through its cobblestone streets, you'll stumble across various areas that seem to have stopped in time, capturing the civilizations that have lived in the city throughout the centuries. You'll see many of València's historical landmarks in this area, including the València Cathedral and La Lonja de la Seda. There is so much historical significance in the old town of València that you'll find yourself whisked away in its timeless charm.

València Cathedral

Address: Plaza Reina, 46003, Valencia

Hours of operation

- January 1 to June 30 and October 1 to December 31
  - Monday to Friday: 10:30 a.m. to 6:30 p.m. (the last admission is at 5:30 p.m.)
  - Saturday: 10:30 a.m. to 5:30 p.m. (the last admission is at 4:30 p.m.)
  - Sunday: 2 p.m. to 5:30 p.m. (the last admission is at 4:30 p.m.)
- July 1 to September 30
  - Monday to Saturday: 10:30 a.m. to 6:30 p.m.
  - Sunday: 2 p.m. to 6:30 p.m.
  - The last admission is at 5:30 p.m. daily

The rich history of València Cathedral dates back to the 13th century and took until the 15th century to complete, resulting in a stunning blend of architectural styles, including Gothic, Romanesque, Baroque, and more. However, even beyond those blended styles, the cathedral's site stems back even further as it once was where a mosque was before it transitioned to a Roman temple, which is something else you'll be able to see in the shape of the church.

As you enter the cathedral, you will find solace in its stunning interior, which features ornate chapels, religious artwork and frescos, and other intricate details. One of the most famous features of València Cathedral is the Santo Caliz Chapel, which is said to hold the chalice Jesus used during the Last Supper. You should also take the time to peruse the museum as it contains a wealth of artifacts, paintings, and sculptures that will give you an insight into València's artistic heritage.

Ticket type	Price
General admission	€ 9
Children (8 to 17 years old) and seniors	€ 6
Children 7 and under	Free
Families (two adults and up to three children)	€ 20

The Miguelete

Hours of operation: 10 a.m. to 6:45 p.m. daily (the last admission is at 6:15 p.m.)

While visiting the València Cathedral, take the time to climb the spiral staircase to the top of the Miguelete Tower (the Bell Tower) to take in the beautiful panoramic views of the city. The construction of this gothic tower began sometime in the 14th century by Andrés Juliá and wasn't completed until the 15th century.

If you intend to climb the tower, please note there are 207 steps to the top.

Ticket type	Price
General admission	€ 2.50
Children (8 to 17 years old) and seniors	€ 1.50
Children 7 and under	Free
Families (two adults and up to three children)	€ 20

La Lonja de la Seda

Address: Lonja 2, 46001 Valencia

Hours of operation

- Monday to Saturday: 10 a.m. to 7 p.m.
- Sunday and public holidays: 10 a.m. to 2 p.m.

La Lonja de la Seda (The Silk Exchange) is a UNESCO World Heritage Site dating back to the 15th century. It was the central trading hub in València and is one of Europe's most famous Gothic monuments. Inside this famous monument, you'll marvel at its intricate stone carvings, grand halls, central tower, and twisted columns. This is such an impressive building, whether you are a history buff or someone who enjoys admiring fine architecture.

The cost of visiting La Lonja de la Seda is €2 per person, but it's free on Sundays and public holidays.

Central Market

Address: Placa Ciutat de Bruges, s/n, 46001 Valencia

Hours of operation: 7:30 a.m. to 3 p.m., Monday to Saturday

Situated behind La Lonja de la Seda is the Central Market, or Mercado Central, Europe's largest market with delicious fresh produce, seafood, meat, spices, and fish.

Even if you're not buying anything, immersing yourself in its vibrant atmosphere is worth 30 minutes, as you can admire the architecture of the building or see the live eels that catch the attention of everyone visiting the market.

Jardí del Turia

Address: Jardines del Turia s/n, 46010 Valencia

Hours of operation: The park is open daily from 10 a.m. to 8 p.m. except for July and August when it is open from 10 a.m. to 2 p.m. and 5 p.m. to 9 p.m.

Jardí del Turia (Turia Gardens) is a stunning urban park through Valencia. This park follows the former route of the Turia River, which had been diverted following a devastating flood in 1957. This park is about five miles long and offers visitors the opportunity to enjoy its lush green spaces, walk its footpaths, and admire the beautifully landscaped gardens filled with palm trees, orange trees, plants, flowers, and ponds. Additionally, this park has 18 bridges displaying different architectural styles from various centuries, which will make for great photos.

This is a beautiful place to picnic in the summer and simply enjoy being in a nature space in the heart of València, a small break from the hustle and bustle of this historic Spanish city.

What Festivals to Enjoy in València

La Fallas de València Festival

Las Fallas de València Festival is a fun celebration to attend as it combines artistic expression, cultural heritage, and communal festivities for you to enjoy along with the locals of this city. This festival, on the UNESCO Intangible Cultural Heritage List, takes place annually in mid-March and incorporates many elements into this ancient tradition of celebrating the incoming spring season. This festival has pre-Christianity origins and has since transformed into a huge event, drawing thousands of locals and tourists to enjoy the festivities. At this festival, you can appreciate the intricate sculptures (fallas) designed by local artists that celebrate or portray a particular theme. Some fireworks and parades last well into the night, making it a big party! On the final day, most of the fellas will be burned to mark the end of the event.

Gran Fira de València

The Gran Fira de València festival takes place in July for over two weeks and has over 100 activities. You can expect to see plenty of live music, performances, fireworks, and various cultural exhibitions during this event. One of this festival's highlights is the flower battle, where you can watch and learn how these float makers masterfully work with flowers in Manises Square.

Day of Valèncian Community

The Day of Valèncian Community is a significant celebration in València to celebrate the day King James I of Aragon entered the city in 1238, ending the Moorish rule. This festival takes place annually on October 9 with plenty of things to experience, including a parade where the flag is taken down from city hall and through the streets to bring it to King James I's monument, then back to city hall and fireworks.

Festival of San Vincente Mártir

The Festival of San Vincente Mártir is one of València's most significant cultural and religious celebrations. It commemorates the martyrdom of Saint Vincent, the city's patron saint, on January 22. You can immerse yourself in spiritual rituals and cultural traditions during this event, beginning at the cathedral. If you don't want to attend the mass, line the streets around 11:30 a.m., as a procession will occur, and follow a route associated with San Vincente.

Where to Eat in València

Did you know Valencia is the birthplace of the famous paella dish? Interestingly, this dish was considered a peasant dish, traditionally prepared by farmers and field laborers using simple and readily available ingredients, often including rice, vegetables, and whatever meat or seafood was accessible.

Over time, this delectable dish has evolved and gained international popularity, becoming a symbol of Spanish cuisine. But if you're looking for some authentic and simple paella, València is where you will find it, among other delicious dishes that incorporate other cuisines.

Canalla Bistro

Address: Calle Maestro Jose Serrano 5, 46005 Valencia

Canalla Bistro is a trendy and modern restaurant offering an exciting menu influenced by many cuisines. This restaurant is on the higher end of options, but with the bold flavors and textures of the dishes, it's worth every euro!

La Riua

Address: Calle Mar 27 46003, 46003 Valencia

La Riua is a lovely little restaurant where you can expect to enjoy traditional Valencian cuisine. People love this place because it has a cozy atmosphere, and they serve plenty of Spanish favorites, including paella. The prices are great here, too, if you're trying to avoid breaking the bank!

Restaurante Canela

Address: Calle Quart 49 También tienen taberna en la misma calle, 46001 Valencia

Restaurante Canela is an excellent option for places catering to vegetarian and vegan dietary needs. This restaurant is nestled in the city's heart and presents and offers a great range of food options. However, this is a great place to go if you are vegan or vegetarian. You can expect prices to be about moderate.

Bodega Casa Montaña

Address: Calle José Benlliure, 69, 46011 València

Bodega Casa Montaña is one of València's oldest restaurants, dating back to 1836. This restaurant is famous for its delicious tapas, which satisfy any craving, including cured meats, seafood, and cheese. Additionally, they have a vast wine list you can enjoy as a sample to pair with your tapas, by the glass, or by the bottle. The prices here are low to moderate, depending on what you order.

Ell Rall

Address: Calle Fundidores 2, 46001 Valencia

For an authentic Valencian meal experience, check out Ell Rall. This restaurant serves delicious tapas and is renowned for its paella. Not feeling paella? Don't worry! Plenty of other great delicacies to explore, including great seafood dishes! You can expect the prices to be about moderate at this restaurant.

What to Eat in València

Paella Valenciana

Valencia is the birthplace of paella, one of Spain's most iconic dishes. Paella Valenciana traditionally includes rabbit, chicken, green beans, and sometimes snails, all cooked together with saffron-infused rice in a wide, shallow pan. The result is a flavorful and aromatic rice dish that captures the essence of the region.

Fideuà

Fideuà is a noodle dish similar to paella but made with short, thin noodles instead of rice. It often features a mix of seafood such as shrimp, mussels, and squid, cooked with noodles in a rich broth. Like paella, it's seasoned with saffron and other aromatic spices.

All i Pebre

All i Pebre is a traditional Valencian dish made with eel, potatoes, garlic, and paprika. The ingredients are slow-cooked in a clay pot with olive oil and the region's distinctive paprika, resulting in a savory and hearty dish.

Orxata de Xufa

Valencia is famous for its horchata, a refreshing and sweet drink made from tiger nuts (chufas). Orxata de Xufa is a cold, milky beverage that is particularly popular during the warm months. Enjoy it on its own or paired with a traditional pastry called fartón.

Arroz a Banda

Another rice dish worth trying in Valencia is Arroz a Banda. This dish consists of rice cooked in a flavorful broth made from fish, squid, and other seafood. It is typically served with a side of aioli (garlic mayonnaise) and showcases the region's emphasis on fresh seafood.

Where to Stay in València

Caro Hotel

Address: Almirante, 14, Ciutat Vella, 46003 Valencia

Caro Hotel is a luxury accommodation option set in a former 19th-century palace, though some parts of this hotel date back even further! In this unique accommodation, the rooms reflect a minimalist look. However, throughout the hotel, you can take in its history with its Roman mosaic dating back to the second century and Arabic walls dating back to the 13th century. This hotel is within walking distance of the València Cathedral and the medieval market.

The Westin València

Address: Calle Amadeo de Saboya 16, 46010 Valencia

The Westin Valencia is a perfect place to stay if you want to be central to everything in València. This hotel's rooms are spacious, with some overlooking their stunning garden. There is also a fitness center and a spa if you want to indulge in self-care while on vacation.

Casual Vintage València

Address: Calle Barcelonina 1, Ciutat Vella, 46002 Valencia

Casual Vintage València is a beautiful accommodation that is both affordable and stylish and is central to several of Vaència's attractions. Travelers have loved staying at this hotel for its vintage theme and because it is a great spot to watch the fireworks.

El Micalet Apartments

Address: Pl. de l'Ajuntament, 25, Ciutat Vella, 46002 València

The El Micalet apartments are a self-catering option in the city's heart. These apartments will put you within walking distance of València's attractions, including the City of Arts and Science. These comfortable apartments will make you feel like you're right at home as they feature all of the basic amenities you would need for your stay, including a fully-equipped kitchen and a washing machine for laundry.

Melia Plaza València:

Address: Plaza del Ayuntamiento, 4, Ciutat Vella, 46002 Valencia

Melia Plaza València is a luxury option in the city's heart, offering a combination of elegance and comfort for your stay. This hotel overlooks the Plaza del Ayuntamiento, putting you central to València's main attractions, including the cathedral and Central Market. If you venture up to their rooftop terrace, you'll be rewarded with panoramic city views. All rooms are tastefully decorated, feature a minibar, and have 24-hour room service. The restaurant on-site also offers gluten-free options.

Primus València

Address: Menorca, 22, Camins al Grau, 46023 València

Hotel Primus Valencia brings relaxation to start and end your day exploring the city. This hotel is well-known and loved for its contemporary architecture, upscale amenities, well-designed and beautifully decorated rooms, and comfortable furnishings. The Hotel Primus València has a beautiful spa and wellness center if you want to indulge in self-care. There are plenty of room options, including ones that will accommodate families.

VLC Mercat Central Flats

Address: 20 Carrer d'Eixarchs, Ciutat Vella, 46001 Valencia

The VLC Mercat Central Flats are a self-catering option to explore. These apartments are central to València's attractions, including the Central Market and the Jardín del Turia. There are different-sized apartments to suit your needs, and they are all equipped with a toaster, coffee machine, fridge, stove, and kettle.

Hotel Neptuno

Address: Paseo de Neptuno, 2, Poblats Maritims, 46011 Valencia

If you seek a beachfront escape for your travels and adventures through València, check out the Hotel Neptuno. This hotel overlooks Malvarrosa Beach, offering stunning views of the Mediterranean Sea and a relaxing atmosphere to start and end your day. Hotel Neptuno is within proximity to several of the city's attractions and restaurants as well.

Hotel RH Sorolla Centro

Address: Convento Santa Clara, 5, Ciutat Vella, 46002 Valencia

Hotel RH Sorolla Centro is in the heart of València, offering simple rooms with contemporary furnishings. This hotel is close to several city attractions, including the Plaza del Ayuntamiento. If you didn't rent a car but need one for the day, this hotel can help you arrange this. This hotel is only available to adult travelers, and you have a choice of rooms between one with a balcony and one without.

One Shot Palacio Reina Victoria 04

Address: Barcas, 4, Ciutat Vella, 46002 Valencia

One Shot Palacio Reina Victoria 04 combines elegance and history in a beautifully restored historical building. This hotel's rooms have been tastefully decorated with contemporary amenities to suit your needs. This hotel is a 10-minute from the cathedral, among other València landmarks. Breakfast is also included with your room fee, and several room options are available.

What Not to Do in València

Don't Stay on the Outskirts of València

If you are looking for other accommodation ideas besides those I've recommended, avoid looking at places in the Nazaret, Orriols, Mislata, Benicalap, Cami Real, and La Coma neighborhoods. Many of these areas have limited accommodation options or are not built well for the tourist infrastructure to travel to landmarks easily. Some of the places are also a little rough.

Don't Buy Separate Tickets in City of Arts and Science

Some attractions within the City of Arts and Sciences offer combination tickets, allowing access to multiple venues at a discounted rate. Avoid overpaying by checking for combination ticket options that suit your interests and itinerary.

Don't Evening Events in City of Arts and Science

The City of Arts and Sciences often hosts evening events, including concerts, performances, and special exhibitions. Avoid missing out on unique experiences by checking the event calendar and considering attending an evening event during your visit.

Don't Miss Exploring Side Streets in Casco Historico

While the main thoroughfares of the Casco Histórico are charming, don't overlook the narrow side streets and alleys, which often hide hidden gems, local shops, and traditional cafes. Avoid sticking only to the main tourist routes and take the time to wander and explore off the beaten path.

Don't Miss to Visit the Holy Grail Chapel at Valencia Cathedral

The Valencia Cathedral is said to house the Holy Chalice, believed by some to be the Holy Grail. Avoid missing this significant relic by visiting the Chapel of the Holy Chalice and learning about its history and significance.

Don't Expect Accessibility Facilities at the Miguelete

The Miguelete Tower has a narrow spiral staircase leading to the top, which may not be suitable for individuals with mobility issues or claustrophobia. Avoid disappointment by checking the accessibility of the tower and its facilities before visiting.

Don't Forget to Carry Cash While Visiting Central Market

While many vendors in the Central Market accept credit and debit cards, some may prefer cash, especially for small purchases. Avoid inconvenience by bringing cash in euros to make transactions easier.

Save Some Appetite While Visiting Central Market

The Central Market is a culinary paradise with numerous stalls selling fresh produce, meats, cheeses, and pastries. Avoid missing out on delicious breakfast options by arriving hungry and sampling some of the market's offerings.

Next Stop: San Sebastián

The captivating city of València will leave you in awe with its ancient roots, stunning landscape, and unique heritage. From exploring the enchanting corners of València's old town to immersing yourself in science and art at the City of Arts and Sciences, there are plenty of things to do and experience in this ancient and enchanting city.

In the next chapter, we will travel to northern Spain to explore San Sebastián, which is well-loved for its beaches, architecture, and delicious cuisine.

Chapter 10:

San Sebastian—Dos and Don'ts

SPAIN

S an Sebastián is nestled within the Bay of Biscay, creating an enchanting backdrop in this northern region of Spain, Donostia. In this town, you'll find a stunning landscape with shorelines that will take your breath away, rich architecture, and delicious cuisine.

Discovering San Sebastián

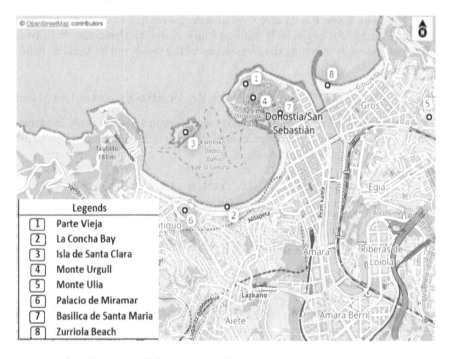

Legends

1	Parte Vieja
2	La Concha Bay
3	Isla de Santa Clara
4	Monte Urgull
5	Monte Ulia
6	Palacio de Miramar
7	Basilica de Santa Maria
8	Zurriola Beach

In San Sebastián, you will be captivated by its stunning landscape, history, and charming elements within the Bay of Biscay. Its history dates back to at least 1014. However, its popularity didn't grow until the 19th century when the Spanish Royal family frequently visited to enjoy bathing in the salt water. Today, it's popular for people looking to enjoy the beaches while enjoying the rich history and admiring famous landmarks and architecture seamlessly woven together.

While visiting this part of Spain, you will notice that several locals speak Basque and Spanish. Interestingly, it is the oldest European language, and its origin remains a mystery to historians! But it is beautiful nonetheless!

This historical city has many charming elements along its narrow, cobblestoned streets, which give a glimpse into its former life. Let's find out what you should do while in San Sebastián.

What to Do in San Sebastián

Parte Vieja

Parte Vieja, San Sebastián's historic old town, stepped into history along its narrow streets. This is one of the most atmospheric areas to explore and immerse yourself in, especially in the evenings, thanks to its many bars and restaurants. However, suppose the nightlife isn't your vibe. In that case, you can still find plenty of things to see in this part of San Antonio, including admiring several parts of Basque architecture and wandering through bustling shopping areas. Some of the noteworthy buildings to admire include

- Plaza de la Constitución was once a place for bullfighting.
- the Church of San Vincente, San Sabastian's oldest building.
- City Hall, which was once a casino.

La Concha Bay

Thanks to its picturesque surroundings, La Concha Bay is San Sebastián's most favored beach and area. Nestled between the mountains of Urgull and Igeldo, La Concha Bay has a crescent-shaped beach with stunning sand and crystal-clear water—everything you would want for a picture-perfect beach day in a Spanish city. When you arrive at La Concha Bay, you will be rewarded with a stunning panorama of the surrounding area. Be sure to walk along the iconic promenade that follows the shoreline and leads to many other restaurants and attractions.

Isla de Santa Clara

One of San Sebastián's claims to fame is having an island right in the middle of its bay. This island is the Isla de Santa Clara and is only 500 meters off of La Concha's coast, making it easily accessible if you rent a boat, kayak, or stand-up paddleboard to get there. This island has plenty of stunning greenery to enjoy a picnic on, and you should check out the lighthouse, which is at the end of a winding path.

Monte Urgull

Monte Urgull has a significant military history, dating back to the 12th century when it was transformed into the Castillo de la Mota fortress to defend San Sebastián due to its strategic location. This is an excellent place for outdoor enthusiasts, as plenty of hiking trails will reward you with spectacular views of the bay. When you reach the top of the mountain, you will see the fortress, home to a small museum with some artifacts on display, which is a free attraction.

Aside from its historical sieges, Monte Urgull is home to some mystery, too. If you follow the Paseo Nuevo walkway, you'll come across an English cemetery where

legend says English soldiers were laid to rest during the First Carlist War; others think the graves are of those belonging to the French soldiers. Whatever is true, you can still get an idea of how the battles impacted this Spanish city all of those years ago.

Monte Ulía

Monte Ulía is another excellent place for outdoor enthusiasts to roam and explore. Between the Ulía and Gros districts, this hill has many trails and hills to hike or bike along. Many of these will lead you to discover much of San Sebastián's former life. While walking along the trails, visit the Peña del Ballenero, a former whaling watchtower. This viewpoint will allow you to take picturesque views of the bay and the city.

Palacio de Miramar

Address: Paseo de Miraconcha 48, 20007 Donostia – San Sebastián

Hours of operation: 7 a.m. to 9 p.m. daily

Palacio del Miramar has plenty of Spanish royal history within its walls and gardens. This beautiful palace dates back to 1887 and was once the summer residence of Queen María Cristina. Today, it serves as a cultural monument and a place to enjoy the simple things in life within its beautifully landscaped gardens while taking in the beautiful scenic views of the Bay of Biscay. Unfortunately, if you want to see inside the building, it's usually closed unless there is a special event.

Basílica de Santa María del Coro

Address: 31 de Agosto Kalea, 46, 20003 Donostia, Gipuzkoa

Hours of operation: 10 a.m. to 1 p.m. and 4 p.m. to 7 p.m. daily

The Basílica de Santa María del Coro is one of San Sebastián's most important 18th-century landmarks. It was built on the site of a former Roman church, the Basílica de Santa María del Coro. This church has a stunning blend of Renaissance and Baroque architecture, reflecting the years it took to build. Inside the church, you will see impressive detailing and religious artwork along its walls. Admission to explore this church is free.

Zurriola Beach

Zurriola Beach is on the other side of Monte Urgull and is a hot spot for surfers due to its impressive waves. If you're a surfer, you will want to visit San Sebastián during the fall or winter, as that is when the best swells roll in at Zurriola. However, even if you don't surf, you can still enjoy the beach, swim safely, or play a volleyball game at one of their beach volleyball courts.

What Festivals to Enjoy in San Sebastián

Tamborrada

Tamborrada in San Sebastián is an exciting and important celebration that takes place annually on January 20. At this festival, thousands of locals gather to participate in a lively drumming festival, transforming the streets into a mix of beats and melodies. This event dates back to the Peninsular War when Napoleon's armies invaded San Sebastián and set a significant amount of the city on fire. The French soldiers also marched through the streets banging on drums, and at some point, the women tasked with getting water from the fountains to help with the fires started to bang back to make fun of the French troops.

This is San Sebastián's biggest party and a great way to immerse yourself in the local culture of San Sebastián.

Olatu-Talka Festival

The Olatu-Talka Festival began in 2010 and is a relatively new festival in San Sebastián that celebrates the city's diverse art and spirit. This late-spring festival offers many cultural activities, including concerts, art installations, and workshops.

St. Thomas Day

St. Thomas Day happens annually on December 21, transforming San Sebastián into a massive market. Hundreds of stalls sell homemade gifts, fresh produce, and more during this festival.

Semana Grande

Semana Grande is a week-long celebration in the middle of August. This festival allows you to immerse yourself in Basque culture and heritage with concerts, a fireworks competition, and Basque athletic events.

Where to Eat in San Sebastián

San Sebastián is well-known for its famous Basque cuisine, characterized by its simple dishes with fresh ingredients that bring the flavors to life on your tastebuds. In San Sebastián, plenty of seafood and fish dishes follow the traditional Basque style and are served in small portions called pintxos (similar to tapas).

La Cuchara de San Telmo

Address: Calle 31 de Agosto, 28, San Sebastián – Donostia
La Cuchara de San Telmo is a delightful restaurant nestled in the heart of San Sebastián's old town. It is popular among locals and visitors for its cozy atmosphere, authentic Basque pintxos, and other delicious small bites made with locally sourced ingredients. The dishes are well within budget, allowing diners to indulge and enjoy the different flavors of Basque.

Gandarias Jatetxea

Address: C/ 31 de Agosto, 23, 20003 San Sebastian – Donostia
Gandarias Jatetxea is another excellent option to experience traditional pintxos in San Sebastián's old town. At this restaurant, you can expect to enjoy an array of bite-sized dishes showcasing the rich flavors and culinary heritage of this part of Spain, all of which you can pair with one of the wines from their expansive list. The

prices here are low to mid-range, so you won't need to worry about breaking your budget!

A Fuego Negro

Address: Calle 31 de agosto, San Sebastián – Donostia
At A Fuego Negro, you will find plenty of Basque cuisine created with an imaginative twist. This restaurant stands out for its innovative approach to traditional Basque dishes, using a fusion of flavors and blending local ingredients with international influences. Diners are always pleasantly surprised by the visually stunning presentation of their pintxos and enjoy the vibrant ambiance as they eat.

Asador Etxebarri

Address: Plaza de San Juan, 1 Axpe, Axpe Achondo
For a Michelin-starred dining experience, many food enthusiasts enjoy eating at Asador Etxebarri. This restaurant is renowned for its steak and other delicious dishes made with locally sourced ingredients. The rustic charm and picturesque surroundings of Asador Etxebarri will also add to your overall dining experience.

Akelaŕe

Address: Paseo del Padre Orcolaga 56, Donostia / San Sebastián, 20008
At Akelaŕe, you can tap into your inner foodie with masterfully crafted dishes showcasing chef Pedro Subjana's love of cooking. This three-star Michelin restaurant has some of the best Basque cuisine, with incredible bay views to enhance your dining experience.

Where to Eat in San Sebastián

Pintxos

San Sebastian is famous for its pintxos, the Basque Country's version of tapas. These small, flavorful bites are served on skewers or toothpicks and range from simple combinations like olives and anchovies to more elaborate creations with seafood, cured meats, and cheeses. Head to the Old Town to explore numerous pintxos bars and enjoy a variety of these delicious bites.

Txangurro

Txangurro is a traditional Basque dish made with spider crab meat, typically mixed with onion, green peppers, and tomatoes. The mixture is then stuffed into crab shells and baked. It's a rich and savory seafood delicacy that showcases the region's maritime flavors.

Codfish in Basque Sauce

Bacalao a la Vizcaína is a popular Basque dish featuring salted codfish cooked in a sauce made with red peppers, onions, garlic, tomatoes, and sometimes almonds. The resulting dish is hearty and flavorful, highlighting the Basque talent for preparing seafood.

Where to Stay in San Sebastián

One Shot Tabakalera House

Address: Paseo Duque de Mandas, 52 (Tabakalera), 20012 San Sebastián

One Shot Tabakalera House is an exciting and budget-friendly accommodation option as it is set in a former tobacco factory. This boutique hotel has a comforting atmosphere: spacious, bright rooms with contemporary furnishings. This accommodation is steps from San Sebastián's old town, among other landmarks, including La Concha beach.

Koisi Hostel

Address: Paseo de Heriz 38, 20008 San Sebastián

If you're traveling solo around Spain or are on a tight budget, check out the Koisi Hostel. At this hostel, you can stay in a private or shared dormitory at affordable rates. This hostel also has a social and communal space where you can mingle with other guests or enjoy pintxos in their rooftop terrace restaurant. This hostel is near several landmarks and attractions, including La Concha Beach and Zurriola Beach.

Pensión Altair

Address: Padre Larroca, 3 , Entresuelo, Gros, 20001 San Sebastián

Pensión Altair is a great-budget-friendly option in San Sebastián's old town. This two-star hotel offers simple, modern rooms as a welcoming, relaxing space for your journeys. This hotel is near several of San Sebastián's attractions and landmarks and La Concha Beach.

Barceló Costa Vasca

Address: Avenida de Pío Baroja, 15, 20008 San Sebastián

Barceló Costa Vaca is a great mid-range accommodation option near many of San Sebastián's landmarks and attractions. This hotel boasts bright rooms with modern amenities and has plenty of facilities to enhance your stay, including a gym and an outdoor swimming pool. Getting to the city center is a short 30-minute walk. However, public transportation is also under a mile away. This hotel has plenty of room options, including ones that can accommodate traveling families.

Room Mate Gorka

Address: 11 Gipuzkoa Plaza, 20004 San Sebastián

Room Mate Gorka is a four-star accommodation in the heart of San Sebastián. This sleek hotel has stunning and stylish rooms with vibrant and innovative decor. Staying here will put you within a distance of San Sebastián's old town and nearby landmarks, including Miramar Palace. If you travel with your family, this hotel is an adult-only accommodation.

Hotel Niza

Address: Barcelona, 23, 43840 Salo

Hotel Niza is a great option to stay near the beach. This one-star hotel offers bright and spacious rooms to relax in. It is steps from La Concha beach. This hotel has many room options, including a family room, without breaking the bank.

Akelarre

Address: Padre Orcolaga 56 Monte Igueldo (San Sebastián), 20008 San Sebastián

Akelarre offers supreme luxury for your Spanish vacation. This hotel boasts stunning rooms, many offering breathtaking ocean views, a walk-in closet, and a private pool. If you want to indulge in wine tasting, this can also be arranged at Akelarre.

Hotel Villa Soro

Address: Avenida de Ategorrieta, 61, Gros, 20013 San Sebastián

If you want to stay in an accommodation that does not look like a hotel, check out the Hotel Villa Soro. This hotel is housed in a restored 19th-century home, offering an elegant retreat while keeping you close to San Sebastián's city center and the beaches. In addition to individually designed rooms, you'll find a fitness center on the property. They also offer complimentary bicycles and beach towels.

Hotel de Londres y de Inglaterra

Address: Zubieta, 2, 20007 San Sebastián

Hotel de Londres y de Inglaterra is a four-star accommodation overlooking La Concha Bay. This hotel is in a 19th-century building, providing modern comfort within its elegant interior and exterior. Many of this hotel's rooms come with stunning ocean views. Staying here will put you within walking distance of many of San Sebastián's other landmarks and attractions.

Olarain

Address: Ondarreta, 24, 20018 San Sebastián

Olarain is an excellent place to stay, especially for younger travelers or if you're extending your stay in San Sebastián. This self-catering option is suitable for different budgets and is near public transportation. You can use the on-site fitness center and multi-use sports courts. Even if you won't be in San Sebastián for long, Olarain is budget-friendly and puts you in the university scene.

What Not to Do in San Sebastián

Don't Underestimate the Waves

Many of San Sebastian's beaches are tucked within The Bay of Biscay. However, you'll want to be mindful of the beaches closest to the Atlantic Ocean, as the waves can get big and dangerous. You'll notice warnings in place to ensure your safety, but be aware of them!

Don't Expect Beach Bathrooms to Be Open All Day

If you spend the day at the beach, especially with young ones, you'll want to ensure you're there when the bathrooms open. During siesta times, bathrooms are most likely closed to the public, so you won't be able to access them.

Don't Miss Water Activities at La Concha Bay

La Concha Bay is an excellent location for water activities such as swimming, paddleboarding, kayaking, and surfing. Avoid missing out on these recreational opportunities by renting equipment or booking a guided activity to explore the bay from a different perspective.

Don't Overlook Boat Schedules at Isle de Santa Clara

Isla de Santa Clara is accessible only by boat, which operates on a schedule. Avoid missing the last boat back to the mainland by checking the departure times in advance and planning your visit accordingly.

Don't Underestimate Hike at Monte Urgull

Monte Urgull offers stunning views of San Sebastian, but the hike to the summit can be steep and challenging for some visitors. Avoid fatigue by wearing comfortable shoes and pacing yourself during the ascent.

Don't Ignore Surf Conditions at Zurriola Beach

Zurriola Beach is known for its excellent surfing conditions, but the waves can vary depending on tides, wind, and other factors. Avoid disappointment or accidents by checking surf reports and assessing conditions before entering the water, especially if you're inexperienced.

San Sebastián is one of the most gorgeous coastal cities in Spain. It is a great place to visit, especially if you want to soak up the Spanish sun while immersing yourself in some of San Sebastián's former life. Whether you love the great outdoors or want to take in some rich architecture, there is plenty to see and do in San Sebastián (and all of Spain).

SPAIN

Conclusion

P lanning a trip does not need to be an overwhelming experience when you know what you want to do and where to go. In this book, we explored many of Spain's most iconic cities, their essential landmarks, and the many festivals each city puts on throughout the year.

With this book, you now have all the information you need to start your trip planning. What stood out the most? Are there some things that are on your must-visit bucket list? If you haven't already, take the time to review and bookmark all the places you'd like to see based on how long you plan to be in Spain. Once your entire trip is planned, all you have to do is get out there and enjoy Spain and everything it has to offer and teach you!

If this book has inspired your trip to Spain, please help other travelers by leaving a review on Amazon.

References

A Coruna. (n.d.). The Hotel Guru. https://www.thehotelguru.com/en-ca/best-hotels-in/spain/a-coruna

Abba Fonseca Hotel. (n.d.). Tripadvisor. https://www.tripadvisor.ca/Hotel_Review-g187493-d231644-Reviews-Abba_Fonseca_Hotel-Salamanca_Province_of_Salamanca_Castile_and_Leon.html

Akelaŕe. (n.d.). Michelin Guide. https://guide.michelin.com/ca/en/pais-vasco/es-donostia-san-sebastian/restaurant/akelare

Akelarre – Relais & Châteaux. (n.d.). Booking.com. https://www.booking.com/hotel/es/akelarre-igueldo.en-gb.html

Aloise, L. (2023a, June 15). An insider's guide to where to stay in Granada in 2023 – the best hotels and Neighborhoods. Spanish Sabores. https://spanishsabores.com/an-insiders-guide-to-where-to-stay-in-granada/#Where_to_Stay_in_Granadas_Historic_Center

Aloise, L. (2023b, July 12). Where to eat in Granada in 2023: The ultimate food guide. Spanish Sabores. https://spanishsabores.com/granada-gastro-guide-where-to-eat-in-granada/#Where_to_Eat_in_Granada_-_The_Best_Tapas_Bars_Restaurants_Cafes

Angan, D. (2022, May 15). Things to know before you go to Cádiz. Culture Trip. https://theculturetrip.com/europe/spain/articles/10-facts-about-cadiz-you-should-know

Anna. (2023a, May 8). 40 best restaurants in Valencia in 2024 (From a Local!). Spain Inspired. https://spaininspired.com/best-restaurants-valencia

Anna. (2023b, June 3). 10 most dangerous areas in Barcelona (2024) - Where to avoid. Spain Inspired. https://spaininspired.com/dangerous-areas-barcelona

Anna. (2023c, June 18). 50 things you should avoid in Barcelona (tourist dos and don'ts!). Spain Inspired. https://spaininspired.com/what-avoid-barcelona

Archaeological and History Museum of A Coruña. (n.d.). Museos de Galicia. https://museos.xunta.gal/en/arqueoloxico-coruna

Art and culture in Spain. (n.d.). Español Spain's Official Tourism Website. https://www.spain.info/en/discover-spain/data-spain-culture/

Asador Etxebarri. (n.d.). Tripadvisor. https://www.tripadvisor.ca/Restaurant_Review-g680977-d877941-Reviews-Asador_Etxebarri-Axpe_Achondo_Province_of_Vizcaya_Basque_Country.html

Barceló Costa Vasca. (n.d.). Booking.com. https://www.booking.com/hotel/es/costavaca.en-gb.html

Barcelona Carnival. (n.d.). Cultura Popular. https://www.barcelona.cat/culturapopular/en/festivals-and-traditions/barcelona-carnival

Barri Gotic: A guide to exploring Barcelona's Gothic Quarter. (n.d.). Hello Jetlag. https://hellojetlag.com/barri-gotic-barcelona

Basilica Santa María del Coro (Church of the Choir). (n.d.). IZI Travel. https://izi.travel/en/23db-basilica-santa-maria-del-coro-church-of-the-choir/en

Beckenham, L. (2020, December 28). The best hotels in A Corua Spain for every traveller. Culture Trip. https://theculturetrip.com/europe/spain/articles/hotels-in-a-coruna

Best hotels in Valencia. (n.d.). The Telegraph. https://www.telegraph.co.uk/travel/destinations/europe/spain/valencia/hotels

Birtles, K. (2020, August 26). Guide to visiting the golden triangle of art in Madrid. The Real Word. https://www.trafalgar.com/real-word/madrid-art-visit-golden-triangle

Bodega Casa Montaña. (n.d.). València the Official Website. https://www.visitvalencia.com/en/what-to-do-valencia/gastronomy/where-to-eat-restaurant-valencia/bodega-casa-montana

Boutique Hotel OLOM – only adults recommended, Cádiz, Spain. (n.d.). Booking.com. https://www.booking.com/hotel/es/la-catedral-cadiz.en-gb.html

Brief look at Spanish history. (n.d.). UniversalClass. https://www.universalclass.com/articles/self-help/brief-look-at-spanish-history.htm

Briney, A. (2019, August 30). An overview of Spain. ThoughtCo. https://www.thoughtco.com/geography-of-spain-1435527

Cádiz Cathedral: a reflection of the city's Golden Age. (n.d.). Barceló Experiences. https://www.barcelo.com/guia-turismo/en/spain/cadiz/things-to-do/cadiz-cathedral

Carr, R., Delano Smith, C., O'Callaghan, J. F., Koenigsberger, H. G., Viguera, M., Harrison, R. J., Rodriguez, V., Richardson, J. S., Shubert, A., & Ginés, J. V. (2024, January 7). Spain. Encyclopedia Britannica. https://www.britannica.com/place/Spain

Castillo de San Antón. (n.d.). Vive El Camino. https://vivecamino.com/en/a-coruna/castillo-de-san-anton-3462/

Casual Vintage Valencia. (n.d.). Tripadvisor. https://www.tripadvisor.ca/Hotel_Review-g187529-d10151358-Reviews-Casual_Vintage_Valencia-Valencia_Province_of_Valencia_Valencian_Community.html

Catalonia Plaza Mayor Salamanca. (n.d.). Tripadvisor. https://www.tripadvisor.ca/Hotel_Review-g187493-d586907-Reviews-Catalonia_Plaza_Mayor_Salamanca-Salamanca_Province_of_Salamanca_Castile_and_Leon.html

Cathedral. (n.d.). Cathedral Cádiz. https://catedraldecadiz.com/la-catedral

Central Market. (n.d.). Valencia the Official Website. https://www.visitvalencia.com/en/what-to-do-valencia/valencian-culture/monuments-in-valencia/central-market

Choose your visit. (n.d.). Basílica de La Sagrada Família. https://tickets.sagradafamilia.org/en

Clive. (2023a, May 1). *The Plaza de San Juan de Dios in Cádiz*. Visiting Cádiz. https://visitingcadiz.com/the-plaza-de-san-juan-de-dios-in-cadiz

Clive. (2023b, May 10). *The Alameda Apodaca y Marqués de Comillas*. Visiting Cádiz. https://visitingcadiz.com/the-alameda-apodaca-y-marques-de-comillas

Corpus procession. (n.d.). Español Spain's Official Tourism Website. https://www.spain.info/en/calendar/corpus-procession

Corral del Carbon in Granada – the oldest Arab Monument of Granada. (n.d.). LoveGranada.com. https://www.lovegranada.com/monuments/corral-del-carbon

Davidson, L. (2021, April 13). *Salamanca Roman Bridge*. History Hit. https://www.historyhit.com/locations/salamanca-roman-bridge

Day of Madrid celebration (Dos de Mayo). (n.d.). TANDEM. https://www.tandemmadrid.com/blogs/2017/04/english/day-of-madrid-dos-mayo

Day of the Taking of Granada. The conquest of Granada. (n.d.). Granadaporelmundo.com. https://www.granadaporelmundo.com/dia-de-la-toma-de-granada

Detailed history of Sagrada Familia | timeline, events & more. (n.d.). Barcelona Tickets. https://sagradafamilia.barcelona-tickets.com/history-of-sagrada-familia

Día de la Cruz in Granada, 2024: Celebrations and traditions. (n.d.). LoveGranada.com. https://www.lovegranada.com/feasts/dia-cruz

Doorway. (2012, September 3). *Travel Review: A Fuego Negro, San Sebastian, Spain*. In the Doorway. https://inthedoorwaydotcom1.wordpress.com/2012/09/03/travel-review-a-fuego-negro-san-sebastian-spain

Dos and don'ts for visiting Spain. (n.d.). YMT Vacations. https://www.ymtvacations.com/travel-blog/spanish-etiquette

Dos de Mayo — A history of Madrid and Spain. (2023, May 2). Madrid Metropolitan. https://www.madridmetropolitan.com/dos-de-mayo-a-history-of-madrid-and-spain

Easter week in Cadiz. (n.d.). Español Spain's Official Tourism Website. https://www.spain.info/en/calendar/easter-week-cadiz

El Bañuelo, the oldest Arab bath in Granada. (n.d.). Barceló Experiences. https://www.barcelo.com/guia-turismo/en/spain/granada/things-to-do/banos-arabes-el-banuelo

El carnaval del toro (bull carnival). (n.d.). Salamanca. http://www.salamancaemocion.es/en/destinos/ciudad-rodrigo-y-la-frontera/te-interesa/el-carnaval-del-toro-bull-carnival

El Micalet. (n.d.). SingularStays Estancias. https://www.singularstays.com/en/rentals/apartment-valencia-el-micalet-182219.html

El Rall. (n.d.). Tripadvisor. https://www.tripadvisor.ca/Restaurant_Review-g187529-d778031-Reviews-El_Rall-Valencia_Province_of_Valencia_Valencian_Community.html

Elmets, J. (2024, January 7). *Best time to visit Spain: Month-by-Month guide to Spain travel*. Adventure in You. https://www.adventureinyou.com/spain/best-time-to-visit-spain

Encyclopaedia Britannica. (n.d.). Retiro Park. In *Encyclopedia Britannica*. Retrieved January 9, 2024, from https://www.britannica.com/place/Retiro-Park

Euskera and Basque culture. (n.d.). Donostia San Sebastián. https://www.sansebastianturismoa.eus/en/to-do/culture-art-architecture/a-unique-and-original-culture

Everything you need to know about the Fallas in Valencia. (n.d.). València the Official Website. https://www.visitvalencia.com/en/events-valencia/festivities/the-fallas/questions-fallas

Expatica. (2024, August 1). *30 interesting facts about Spain*. https://www.expatica.com/es/moving/about/facts-about-spain-109108

Fergusson, L. (2023, December 14). *27 top Spain packing list items for 2024 + what to wear & not to bring*. Asher & Lyric. https://www.asherfergusson.com/must-have-spain-packing-list-items

Festival of Granada. (n.d.). Español Spain's Official Tourism Website. https://www.spain.info/en/calendar/festival-granada

Festival of Sant Jordi in Barcelona. (n.d.). Español Spain's Official Tourism Website. https://www.spain.info/en/discover-spain/fiesta-sant-jordi-barcelona

Festivities of María Pita. (2014, July 16). Vueling. https://blog.vueling.com/en/inspiration/festivities-of-maria-pita/#:~:text=Throughout%20the%20month%20of%20August,pirate%20Francis%20Drake%20in%201589.

Fox, E. (2018, May 17). *9 things you need to know about Corpus Christi in Spain*. Culture Trip. https://theculturetrip.com/europe/spain/articles/9-things-you-need-to-know-about-corpus-christi-in-spain

Galiwonders. (n.d.). *San Juan night: Spain's bonfire night*. Galiwonders.com. https://galiwonders.com/en/blog/san-juan-night-spains-bonfire-night

Gandarias Jatetxea. (n.d.). Tripadvisor. https://www.tripadvisor.ca/Restaurant_Review-g187457-d2148045-Reviews-Gandarias_Jatetxea-San_Sebastian_Donostia_Province_of_Guipuzcoa_Basque_Country.html

Geography and landscape. (n.d.). Español Spain's Official Tourism Website. https://www.spain.info/en/discover-spain/facts-spain-geography-landscape/

Godoy, S. (2021, September 20). *A brief introduction to Spanish culture, traditions, and beliefs*. Homeschool Spanish Academy. https://www.spanish.academy/blog/a-brief-introduction-to-spanish-culture-traditions-and-beliefs

Goins, D. (2019, August 2). *10 of the best restaurants in Cádiz, Spain*. The Guardian. https://www.theguardian.com/travel/2019/aug/02/10-best-restaurants-cadiz-spain-andalucia-tapas-seafood

Gordon, E. (2016, September 13). *What not to do in Spain*. My Daily Spanish. https://mydailyspanish.com/guide-traveling-spain

Goulding, M. (2016, November 17). *13 things to know before you go to Salamanca*. Roads & Kingdoms. https://roadsandkingdoms.com/2016/salamanca

Gran Fira de València. (n.d.). Amazing Capitals. https://valencia.amazingcapitals.com/event/gran-fira-valencia

Gran Vía, Madrid. (n.d.). Civitatis Madrid. https://www.introducingmadrid.com/gran-via

Great Valencia Fair. (n.d.). València the Official Website. https://www.visitvalencia.com/en/events-valencia/great-valencia-fair

Guide to visiting Madrid's Royal Palace. (2020, January 30). TripSavvy. https://www.tripsavvy.com/el-palacio-royal-1643666

Guided tours and audio guides. (n.d.). Museu Picasso. https://museupicassobcn.cat/en/plan-your-visit/guided-tours-and-audioguides

Gunning, C. (2024, January 2). *Cadiz, Spain: The ultimate travel guide*. Wanderlust Chloe. https://www.wanderlustchloe.com/cadiz-spain-travel-guide

Hansen, M. (2023, September 14). *Where to stay in Barcelona: A complete guide*. Whatless Wanderlust. https://wheatlesswanderlust.com/where-to-stay-barcelona-best-places/?gad_source=1&gclid=CjwKCAiA75itBhA6EiwAkho9e-s5w_IgSuQtpC3-MgAxcALhoaOL2jmP54_71icsIp0LeDfNa7yMyhoCYOEQAvD_BwE

Haydn, J. (1786). *The seven last words of Christ*.

Historic helmet. (n.d.). Zaragoza. https://www.zaragoza.es/sede/portal/turismo/post/casco-historico

History. (n.d.-a). Jaén Castillo de Santa Catalina. https://castillosantacatalina.es/en/history

History. (n.d.-b). Casa Montaña. https://www.emilianobodega.com/en/history

History of Alhambra of Granada. (n.d.). Alhambra.org. https://www.alhambra.org/en/alhambra-history.html

History of Granada. (n.d.). Civitatis Granada. https://en.granada.info/history

History of San Sebastian (Donostia). (n.d.). What San Sebastian. https://www.whatsansebastian.com/donostia-san-sebastian.html

History of Valencia. (n.d.). Valencia the Official Website. https://www.visitvalencia.com/en/what-to-do-valencia/valencian-culture/history

Hotel de Londres y de Inglaterra. (n.d.). Booking.com. https://www.booking.com/hotel/es/londresinglaterra.en-gb.html

Hotel Las Cortes De Cádiz. (n.d.). Kayak. https://www.kayak.com/Cadiz-Hotels-Hotel-Las-Cortes-De-Cadiz.138843.ksp

Hotel Monte Puertatierra. (n.d.). Booking.com. https://www.booking.com/hotel/es/puertatierra.en-gb.html

Hotel Neptuno. (n.d.). Booking.com. https://www.booking.com/hotel/es/neptunovalencia.en-gb.html

Hotel Niza. (n.d.). Booking.com. https://www.booking.com/hotel/es/niza-salou.en-gb.html

Hotel RH Sorolla Centro. (n.d.). Booking.com. https://www.booking.com/hotel/es/sorolla.en-gb.html

Hotel Villa Soro. (n.d.). Booking.com. https://www.booking.com/hotel/es/villasoro.en-gb.html

How to rent a boat in El Retiro Park (Madrid). (n.d.). Madrid Traveling. https://madridtraveling.com/what-to-do/retiro-park-boat-rental

Hudec, D. (2020, December 31). *The Spanish Christmas tradition of Los Reyes Magos*. Speakeasy. https://www.speakeasybcn.com/en/blog/the-spanish-christmas-tradition-of-los-reyes-magos

Jessica. (2018, October 6). *10 essential Spain travel tips for first time visitors*. The Belle Voyage. https://www.thebellevoyage.com/spain-travel-tips

Jessop, T. (2018, April 18). *10 things to know before visiting the Palau de la Musica Catalana*. Culture Trip. https://theculturetrip.com/europe/spain/articles/10-things-to-know-before-visiting-the-palau-de-la-musica-catalana

Juliff, L. (2023, November 1). *How to pack for Spain: My complete packing list for 2023*. Never Ending Footsteps. https://www.neverendingfootsteps.com/spain-packing-list

Kliger, I., & Askham, G. (2023, April 3). *The 32 best hotels in Barcelona*. Condé Nast Traveler. https://www.cntraveler.com/gallery/best-hotels-in-barcelona

Koisi Hostel. (n.d.). Booking.com. https://www.booking.com/hotel/es/koisi-hostel.en-gb.html#map_closed

Komenda, P. (2020, May 13). *10 of the best restaurants to try in Salamanca, Spain*. Culture Trip. https://theculturetrip.com/europe/spain/articles/a-foodie-s-guide-to-salamanca-10-restaurants-you-should-try

La Caleta. (n.d.). Andalusía. https://www.andalucia.org/en/cadiz-sun-and-beaches-la-caleta

La Cuchara de San Telmo. (n.d.). San Sebastián Pintxo Bars. https://sansebastianpintxobars.com/pintxo-bars/la-cuchara-de-san-telmo

La Lonja (The Silk Exchange) Unesco World Heritage. (n.d.). Valencia the Official Website. https://www.visitvalencia.com/en/what-to-do-valencia/valencian-culture/monuments-in-valencia/lonja-silk-exchange

La Riua. (n.d.). Tripadvisor. https://www.tripadvisor.ca/Restaurant_Review-g187529-d897007-Reviews-La_Riua-Valencia_Province_of_Valencia_Valencian_Community.html

Lamberg, E., & Danise, A. (2023, June 30). *Travel insurance: USA to Spain trip*. Forbes Advisor. https://www.forbes.com/advisor/travel-insurance/destinations/spain-trips

Lara. (2023, February 17). *Best places where to stay in Valencia (+ areas to avoid)*. Valencia Revealed. https://www.valenciarevealed.com/where-to-stay-in-valencia

Laura. (2022a, November 7). *9 interesting & fun facts about Granada*. Travelers Universe. https://www.travelersuniverse.com/granada-facts

Laura. (2022b, November 9). *21 interesting & fun facts about Madrid*. Traveler's Universe. https://www.travelersuniverse.com/madrid-facts

Laura. (2023a, February 12). *23 interesting & fun facts about Barcelona*. Traveler's Universe. https://www.travelersuniverse.com/barcelona-facts

Laura. (2023b, February 12). *23 interesting & fun facts about Valencia*. Travelers Universe. https://www.travelersuniverse.com/valencia-facts

Laureano, C. (2023, September 26). *Safety guide: Is Spain safe?* Travel Right. https://travelright.com/safety-guide-is-spain-safe/

Lichtman, A. J. (2021). Obama: Benghazi and Clinton's Emails. *AMERICAN HERITAGE*, 66(2). https://www.americanheritage.com/obama-benghazi-and-clintons-emails

Lobo, J. (2023, June 8). *Discover Picasso's masterpieces at the Barcelona Picasso Museum*. Headout Blog. https://www.headout.com/blog/picasso-museum-barcelona

A locals guide to Bogatell Beach Barcelona. (2017, March 18). Culture Trip. https://theculturetrip.com/europe/spain/articles/a-locals-guide-to-bogatell-beach-barcelona

Lussiana, M. (2021, May 4). *First in at the Mandarin Oriental Ritz, Madrid*. Condé Nast Traveller. https://www.cntraveler.com/article/mandarin-oriental-ritz-madrid-hotel-review

Madrid Spain map, history and culture. (2023, May 9). Map of Us. https://www.mapofus.org/madrid-spain-map

Madrid's Temple of Debod: The complete guide. (n.d.). TripSavvy. https://www.tripsavvy.com/madrid-temple-of-debod-complete-guide-4583163

Marouli, N. (2023, April 24). *Feria Granada: History, dates, and things to do*. South Tours Magazine. https://south.tours/magazine/feria-granada-history-dates-and-things-to-do

Melia Maria Pita. (n.d.). Booking.com. https://www.booking.com/hotel/es/meliamariapita.en-gb.html

Melia Plaza Valencia. (n.d.). Booking.com. https://www.booking.com/hotel/es/melia-plaza.en-gb.html

Mendenhall, K. (2023, November 28). *34 facts about La Coruña*. Facts.net. https://facts.net/world/cities/34-facts-about-la-coruna

Menhires Pola Paz. (n.d.). Atlas Obscura. https://www.atlasobscura.com/places/menhires-pola-paz

Miller, A. (2023, December 4). *Where to stay in Barcelona: 7 neighborhoods and places to stay + best hotels*. WhereToStayIn.City. https://wheretostayin.city/best-places-to-stay-in-barcelona?utm_source=google&utm_medium=cpc&utm_campaign=20917789614&utm_co ntent=686985055621&utm_term=where%20to%20stay%20in%20barcelona&gclid=CjwKC AiA75itBhA6EiwAkho9e44cu56xaxtr4Vo2E8M4yLEAosspZjJF_pD22Kl5JAV7ABRwN_yUo xoC6YYQAvD_BwE

Miller, A. (2024, January 14). *Where to stay in Madrid: Best areas & places to stay*. WhereToStayIn.City. https://wheretostayin.city/best-places-to-stay-in-madrid?utm_source=google&utm_medium=cpc&utm_campaign=20782296719&utm_cont ent=681696552605&utm_term=where%20to%20stay%20in%20madrid%20spain&gclid=Cj

wKCAiAqY6tBhAtEiwAHeRopU4YYc9fVP4HHQwlKVtRUB827sUnCThsDutZET52cAg9e1G
69h_Y-hoCUxoQAvD_BwE

Mimo's Born. (n.d.). Tripadvisor. https://www.tripadvisor.com/Restaurant_Review-g187497-
d17527277-Reviews-Mimo_s_Born-Barcelona_Catalonia.html

Miramar Palace. (n.d.). Euskadi Basque Country. https://tourism.euskadi.eus/en/cultural-
heritage/miramar-palace/aa30-12375/en

Monte Ulía, urban nature. (n.d.). Barceló Experiences. https://www.barcelo.com/guia-
turismo/en/spain/san-sebastian/things-to-do/monte-ulia/

Mount Urgull. (n.d.). Donostia San Sebastian. https://www.sansebastianturismoa.eus/en/to-do/what-
not-to-miss/mount-urgull

Móvil, P. (2023, October 25). *The 38 best restaurants in Madrid.* Eater.
https://www.eater.com/maps/best-madrid-restaurants-38

Museo Art Nouveau y Art Déco Casa Lis. (n.d.). Cityseeker. https://cityseeker.com/salamanca/130726-
museo-art-nouveau-y-art-d%C3%A9co-casa-lis

Museum Casa de Lis. (n.d.). Español Spain's Official Tourism Website.
https://www.spain.info/en/activities/museum-casa-de-lis/

Nayler, M. (2017, November 24). *Everything you need to know about the Cádiz carnival.* Culture Trip.
https://theculturetrip.com/europe/spain/articles/everything-you-need-to-know-about-the-
cadiz-carnival

Nayler, M. (2022, March 4). *The best hotels in Cádiz, Spain for every traveler.* Culture Trip.
https://theculturetrip.com/europe/spain/articles/the-best-hotels-in-cadiz-spain

NH Collection Salamanca Palacio de Castellanos. (n.d.). Tripadvisor.
https://www.tripadvisor.ca/Hotel_Review-g187493-d207001-Reviews-
NH_Collection_Salamanca_Palacio_de_Castellanos-
Salamanca_Province_of_Salamanca_Castile_.html

Nowek, A. (2024, January 8). *Public transport in Spain: trains, trams, and buses.* Expatica for
Internationals. https://www.expatica.com/es/living/transportation/public-transport-spain-
101423

Old city of Salamanca. (n.d.). UNESCO World Heritage Centre. https://whc.unesco.org/en/list/381

One Shot Palacio Reina Victoria 04. (n.d.). Booking.com. https://www.booking.com/hotel/es/one-shot-
palacio-reina-victoria.en-gb.html

One Shot Tabakalera House. (n.d.). Booking.com. https://www.booking.com/hotel/es/one-shot-
tabakalera-house.en-gb.html?aid=311088&label=one-shot-tabakalera-house-pouh

Opening times and prices. (n.d.). Museo Del Prado. https://www.museodelprado.es/en/visit/opening-
times-and-prices

Parte Vieja (Old Town). (n.d.). Donostia San Sebastián.
https://accessibility.sansebastianturismoa.eus/en/to-do/accesible-routes/parte-vieja-old-
town

Pensión Altair. (n.d.). Booking.com. https://www.booking.com/hotel/es/pension-altair.en-gb.html

Perkins, M. (2019, May 20). *Las Fallas de Valencia: Spain's annual festival of fire.* ThoughtCo.
https://www.thoughtco.com/las-fallas-de-valencia-4628348

Plaza de María Pita. (n.d.). A Coruña Tourist Board. https://www.visitcoruna.com/turismo/en/que-
hacer-en-a-coruna/arte-y-cultura/equipamientos/detalle-equipamiento/plaza-de-maria-
pita/entidad/1374541973201?argIdioma=en

Plaza del Humor. (n.d.). Lonely Planet. https://www.lonelyplanet.com/spain/cantabria-asturias-and-
galicia/la-coruna/attractions/plaza-del-humor/a/poi-sig/1298366/1004421

Plaza Mayor. (n.d.-a). Madrid. https://www.esmadrid.com/en/tourist-information/plaza-mayor-madrid

Plaza Mayor. (n.d.-b). Lonely Planet. https://www.lonelyplanet.com/spain/castilla-y-
leon/salamanca/attractions/plaza-mayor/a/poi-sig/484132/360754

Plaza Mayor square in Madrid. (n.d.). Español Spain's Official Tourism Website.
https://www.spain.info/en/places-of-interest/plaza-mayor-madrid

Poellae, L. (2023, November 13). *La Cartuja Monastery in Granada: Is it worth a visit?* Viva La Vita.
https://www.thevivalavita.com/la-cartuja-monastery-granada

Primus Valencia. (n.d.). Booking.com. https://www.booking.com/hotel/es/primus-valencia.en-gb.html

Rabbie. (2023, April 11). *Direct flights to Spain from the USA 2024.* Rabbie's.
https://www.rabbies.com/en/blog/flights/flights-to-spain-from-usa

Rates 2024. (n.d.). La Ciutat. https://cac.es/en/tarifas

RD. (n.d.). *Virgin of Almudena festival in Madrid.* Fascinating Spain.
https://fascinatingspain.com/party-of-spain/spanish-festivities-in-november/madrid-
virgin-of-almudena-festival

Restaurante Canela. (n.d.). Tripadvisor. https://www.tripadvisor.ca/Restaurant_Review-g187529-
d1739724-Reviews-Restaurante_Canela-
Valencia_Province_of_Valencia_Valencian_Community.html

Restaurants in La Coruna. (n.d.). Tripadvisor. https://www.tripadvisor.com/Restaurants-g187507-La_Coruna_Province_of_A_Coruna_Galicia.html

Retiro Park. (n.d.). Madrid Pour Vous. https://madridpourvous.com/en/retiro-park

Roman Theatre of Cádiz (Teatro Romano de Cádiz) tours and tickets. (n.d.). Viator. https://www.viator.com/en-CA/Cadiz-attractions/Teatro-Romano-de-Cadiz/d22439-a21287

Room Mate Gorka. (n.d.). Booking.com. https://www.booking.com/hotel/es/room-mate-gorka.en-gb.html

Saint Vicente Martir Festival in Valencia. (n.d.). València the Official Website. https://www.visitvalencia.com/en/events-valencia/festivities/sant-vicente-martir-festival

Salamanca. (n.d.). The Hotel Guru. https://www.thehotelguru.com/en-ca/best-hotels-in/spain/salamanca

Salamanca festivals. (n.d.). What Salamanca Online Travel Guide. https://www.whatsalamanca.com/salamanca-festival.html

Salamanca hotels and places to stay. (n.d.). Tripadvisor. https://www.tripadvisor.ca/Hotels-g187493-Salamanca_Province_of_Salamanca_Castile_and_Leon-Hotels.html

Salamanca Plaza Mayor Square. (n.d.). Español Spain's Official Tourism Website. https://www.spain.info/en/places-of-interest/plaza-mayor-salamanca

Salamanca Suite Studios. (n.d.). Tripadvisor. https://www.tripadvisor.ca/Hotel_Review-g187493-d6105364-Reviews-Salamanca_Suite_Studios-Salamanca_Province_of_Salamanca_Castile_and_Leon.html

San Anton Castle. (n.d.). Coruña Culture. https://www.coruna.gal/sites/Satellite?pagename=cultura/Page/Generico-Page-Generica&cid=1322783576553&itemID=1149055937727&itemType=Entidad

San Cecilio Festival in Granada – celebrations in honour of the city's Patron Saint. (n.d.). LoveGranada.com. https://www.lovegranada.com/feasts/san-cecilio

San Juan de Sahagún, charro tradition. (2016, June 1). Ábaco Salamanca Spain. https://salamancaspanish.com/en/san-juan-of-sahagun-charro-tradition

San Sebastian city information. (n.d.). UniSpain. https://www.unispain.com/San-Sebastian-City-Information.htm

Santa Clara Island: the sentinel of La Concha Bay. (n.d.). Barceló Experiences. https://www.barcelo.com/guia-turismo/en/spain/san-sebastian/things-to-do/santa-clara-island

Sara. (n.d.). *The worst neighborhoods in Madrid: 10 unsafe areas to avoid.* Madrid Traveling. https://madridtraveling.com/planning/areas-to-avoid-in-madrid

Sears-Piccavey, M. (2018, July 11). *What not to do in Granada Spain – 7 tips to look like a local.* Spain-Holiday.com. https://www.spain-holiday.com/Granada-city/articles/what-not-to-do-granada

Segura, E. (2016, November 28). *Madrid's Golden Triangle: El Prado, Reina Sofia, and Thyssen-Bornemisza.* Culture Trip. https://theculturetrip.com/europe/spain/articles/madrids-golden-triangle-el-prado-reina-sofia-and-thyssen-bornemisza

Semana Santa: 10 top experiences in Madrid at Easter. (n.d.). Pin and Travel. https://www.barcelo.com/pinandtravel/en/top-experiences-semana-santa-in-madrid

Spain tourist visa for visitors. (n.d.). Visaguide.world. https://visaguide.world/europe/spain-visa/tourist-visitor

Spanish currency. (n.d.). Wise. https://wise.com/gb/travel-money/spanish-currency

Speak, C. (2017a, May 15). *10 cultural trends and movements that started in Valencia Spain.* Culture Trip. https://theculturetrip.com/europe/spain/articles/10-cultural-trends-and-movements-that-started-in-valencia-spain

Speak, C. (2017b, June 20). *How to spend 24 hours in Salamanca.* Culture Trip. https://theculturetrip.com/europe/spain/articles/how-to-spend-24-hours-in-salamanca

Stamper, P. (2021a, March 25). *Casa de las Conchas.* History Hit. https://www.historyhit.com/locations/casa-de-las-conchas

Stamper, P. (2021b, May 21). *Valencia Cathedral.* History Hit. https://www.historyhit.com/locations/valencia-cathedral

Star Route Scandal. (n.d.). Academic Accelerator. https://academic-accelerator.com/encyclopedia/star-route-scandal

Star Route scandal facts and worksheets. (2017, August 23). KidsKonnect. https://kidskonnect.com/social-studies/star-route-scandal

Tamborrada. (n.d.). Eusk Guide. https://www.euskoguide.com/festivals-events/tamborrada-san-sebastian-day

Taps. (n.d.). Tripadvisor. https://www.tripadvisor.com/Restaurant_Review-g187497-d7707574-Reviews-Taps-Barcelona_Catalonia.html

Tavira Tower's history. (n.d.). Torre Tavira. https://www.torretavira.com/en/tavira-towers-history

10times. (2023, July 18). *Cultural know-how when visiting Spain.* https://blog.10times.com/cultural-know-how-when-visiting-spain

The architectural innovations in Casa Mila (La Pedrera). (n.d.). La Pedrera — Casa Milá. https://www.lapedrera.com/en/la-pedrera/architecture

The building. (n.d.). Miramar Jauregia Palacio. https://www.miramar.eus/en/the-palace/the-building

The Concha Bay. (n.d.). Donostia San Sebastian. https://www.sansebastianturismoa.eus/en/to-do/what-not-to-miss/the-concha-bay

The Day of the Valencian Community. (n.d.). Drivalia. https://www.drivalia.es/en/the-day-of-the-valencian-community

The Editors of Encyclopaedia Britannica. (n.d.-a). A Coruña. In *Encyclopaedia Britannica.* Retrieved January 19, 2024, from https://www.britannica.com/place/A-Coruna-Spain

The Editors of Encyclopaedia Britannica. (n.d.-b). *Granada.* Encyclopedia Britannica. https://www.britannica.com/place/Granada-Spain#ref256944

The Editors of Encyclopaedia Britannica. (n.d.-c). Paella. In *Encyclopædia Britannica.* Retrieved February 1, 2024, from https://www.britannica.com/topic/paella

The Editors of Encyclopaedia Britannica. (n.d.-d). Spanish Armada. In *Encyclopædia Britannica.* Retrieved January 19, 2024, from https://www.britannica.com/topic/Armada-Spanish-naval-fleet

The Editors of Encyclopaedia Britannica. (n.d.-e). Tower of Hercules. In *Encyclopedia Britannica.* Retrieved January 19, 2024, from https://www.britannica.com/topic/Tower-of-Hercules

The heart of the most cosmopolitan and authentic Madrid. (n.d.). Meliá Madrid Princesa. https://www.melia.com/en/hotels/spain/madrid/melia-madrid-princesa

The Maria Pita Square. (n.d.). Galicia Guide. http://www.galiciaguide.com/Maria-Pita-square.html

The old and new cathedrals of Salamanca. (n.d.). Mapping Spain. https://mappingspain.com/the-old-and-new-cathedrals-of-salamanca/

The only Spain packing list you'll ever need: What to pack for Spain for all seasons. (2019, November 21). Wandertooth. https://www.wandertooth.com/spain-packing-list-what-to-pack-for-spain/#packinglists

The Sacristy-Museum – Royal Chapel of Granada. (n.d.). Capilla Real de Granada. https://capillarealgranada.com/en/the-sacristy-museum

The San Juan bonfires (A Coruña). (n.d.). Español Spain's Official Tourism Website. https://www.spain.info/en/calendar/bonfires-san-juan-a-coruna

30 facts about Spain. (n.d.). Expatica for Internationals. https://www.expatica.com/es/moving/about/facts-about-spain-109108/#second-largest-country

Tips on Cadiz warnings or dangers – stay safe! (2017, February 24). SmarterTravel. https://www.smartertravel.com/tips-cadiz-warnings-dangers-stay-safe

Top 13 festivals in San Sebastian you won't want to miss. (2023, June 28). Devour. https://devourtours.com/blog/festivals-san-sebastian/?cnt=CA

Traveling to Spain? Find La Coruna hotels. (n.d.). Agoda. https://www.agoda.com/city/la-coruna-es.html?cid=1844104&ds=c3O9IHB7SH6n1V9J

Valencia Fallas festivity. (n.d.). UNESCO Intangible Cultural Heritage. https://ich.unesco.org/en/RL/valencia-fallas-festivity-00859

Virtual Tourist. (2017, February 24). *Tips on San Sebastián warnings and dangers—stay safe!* SmarterTravel. https://www.smartertravel.com/tips-san-sebastian-warnings-dangers-stay-safe

Visitable spaces. (n.d.). Catedral de Barcelona. https://catedralbcn.org/visita-turistica/espais-visitables

Visits the Palau. (n.d.). Palau de La Música Catalana. https://www.palaumusica.cat/en/visits-and-tickets_1159168

VLC Mercat Central Flats. (n.d.). Booking.com. https://www.booking.com/hotel/es/vlc-eixarchs-flats.en-gb.html

Wanderlog Staff. (2023, August 16). *Where to eat: The 50 best restaurants in Salamanca.* Wanderlog. https://wanderlog.com/list/geoCategory/74428/where-to-eat-best-restaurants-in-salamanca

Wanderlog staff. (2023, July 26). *Where to eat: The 50 best restaurants in La Coruna.* Wanderlog. https://wanderlog.com/list/geoCategory/74547/where-to-eat-best-restaurants-in-la-coruna

Why visit the Granada Cathedral? (n.d.). Espana Guide. https://www.espanaguide.com/granada/cathedral

Zaino, L. (2018, March 19). *A brief history of the Palacio Real.* Culture Trip. https://theculturetrip.com/europe/spain/articles/a-brief-history-of-the-palacio-real

Zucker, S. (2023, April 7). *The 38 essential Barcelona restaurants.* Eater. https://www.eater.com/maps/best-restaurants-barcelona-spain

Zurriola Beach. (n.d.). U.S. News. https://travel.usnews.com/San_Sebastian_Spain/Things_To_Do/Zurriola_Beach_63634